AF264742

Weaving on the 2ft Square Loom

A Collection of Plaids

Ashli Couch and Theresa Jewell

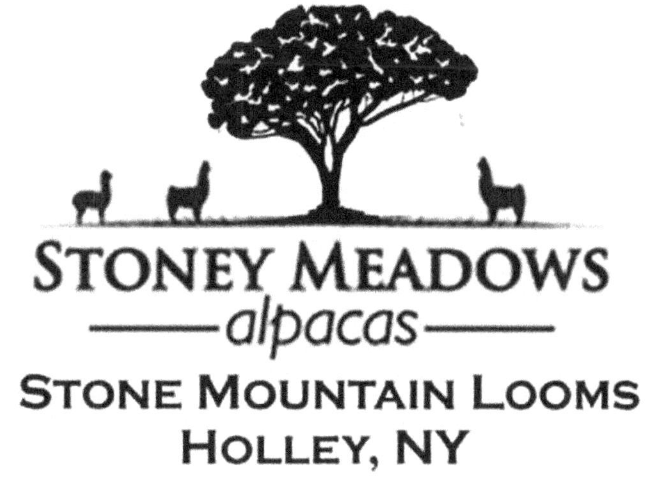

Table of Contents

We dedicate this book

To

Our Nanny

When we needed help the most, Nanny was prepared to pick up a hammer and keep us
moving forward. Thank you for all your support and help, this business really could not
have grown without you!

Welcome!

We are so glad you chose to pick up our second book on weaving on continuous strand looms. It has been quite the journey writing our first book and now with our second here, we are excited to see where we go next. For those of you returning, welcome back, and for those of you just starting, we hope you like what you see and walk away with a better knowledge of your continuous strand loom and of course, beautiful projects.

Before we get started, I'd like to tell you a story.

Once upon a time, there was a young woman just minding her own business at a yarn shop when she heard a familiar voice. Walking around the corner, she came face to face with her surrogate aunt. Her aunt, Theresa, was in the middle of teaching a class on continuous strand weaving on the rectangle loom.

That didn't stop her from looking up, interrupt her class to say hi and give the young woman a big hug. But it didn't stop there. Theresa took her hand, led her to the rectangle loom, and handed her the magic wand, her afghan crochet hook. She then continued to teach the class, using the young woman to demonstrate how easy it was.

That's how I was introduced to continuous strand weaving for the first time. Nothing like learning on the fly and with an audience, yikes! But it was interesting and different. I ended up staying for the entire class and helped Theresa pack her car when she finished. So much for getting pretty yarn to knit with. Whoops.

As usually, we ended up talking awhile in the parking lot and Theresa asked me if I'd like to help her out at a Celtic festival since her sister would be unable to assist this year. Of course I said yes. It's a Celtic festival, who doesn't like Celtic festivals? Between the great food, fabulous music, and amazing company, Celtic festivals are the best.

When the time rolled around for the Celtic festival, I was excited. It turned out to be a blast! We sold a huge number of items, met some great people, froze our butts off, and overall enjoyed ourselves. It was our first time vending together and it was such a huge success that we planned more events together. Well…. more Celtic events together.

Since then, we have participated in a few different Celtic festival events around New York every year. And every year, we create new plaids on our looms to present at the shows. We enjoy making plaids for these events, and decided it was time to share some of them with you!

Over the next few chapters, we will walk you through step-by-step instructions on how to set-up, weave, change colors, some troubleshooting and finish your square looms. Once we get through all that boring, but necessary, stuff you'll find a collection of plaids from Theresa's pattern binder. Each plaid was uniquely designed by Theresa for Stone Mountain Looms, and all examples of the plaids were woven by Theresa or myself.

May you weave many beautiful projects and have fun doing it!

-Ashli

Before you get Started

Before you start your project it's always a good idea to know how much yarn you need. If you're not sure, a good rule of thumb is to purchase more than you need of a particular color of yarn so you have the same dye lot. To complete one panel off the 2ft square loom, you need approximately 250 yards of yarn. This gives you a lot of wiggle room for mistakes, and a final border later.

The way we start and weave on the square looms is the same as how we start on any of our looms: with a slip knot. If you are unsure how to make a slip knot, we have provided a step by step for you on the next page. If you already know how to tie a slip knot, you're ahead of the game and can skip to the next section.

Both Theresa and I are visual learners. Therefore, we will provide as many pictures as we can to help instruct you in starting your loom!

I have used the first pattern, Iris Bouquet on page 40, to demonstrate how to start and finish your loom. My final project for the Iris Bouquet pattern is Design number 1, the Wrap you can find on page 26. Feel free to use a different pattern or design or use scrap yarn to practice.

Here's what my final project looks like!

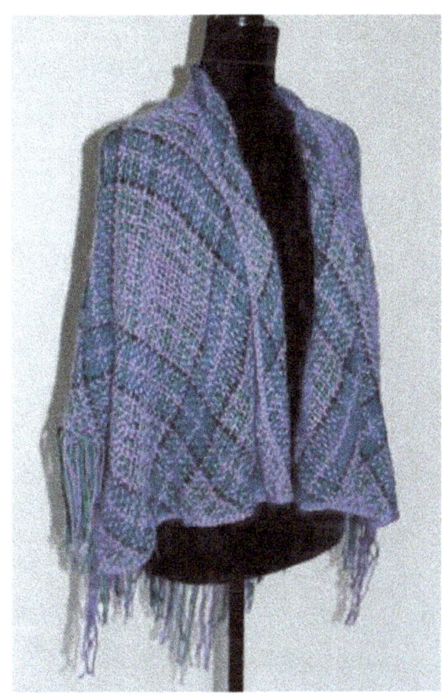

Tying a Slip Knot

A slip knot can be very tricky, but you can do it. We have provided you with an easy step by step guide with pictures to help you with the process.

Step 1: Start by finding the yarn you want to start your project with and find an end. I prefer to work with the 'wrong' end or the end that unravels around the skein of yarn. Others prefer working with the end that pulls from the center of the skein. Start with whichever end you are comfortable with.

Step 2: Pull enough string out for fringe or enough to make you feel comfortable that is long enough for you to handle. You don't want it super long, just a comfortable amount of string. Approximately 12-16 inches will work nicely.

Step 3: Lay your string on a flat surface. Pick up the yarn closest to the skein and make a loop over, near the end of your yarn.

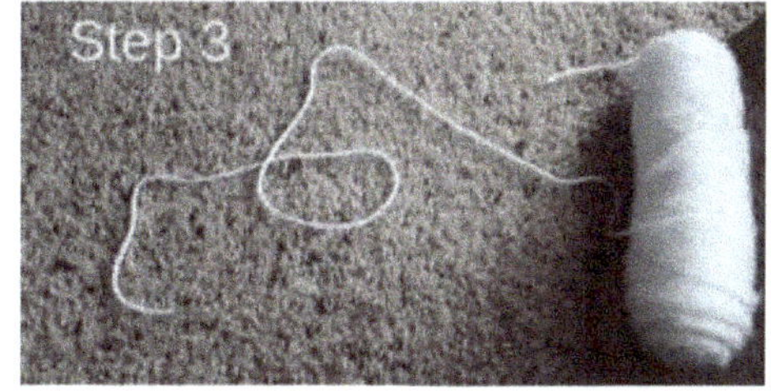

Step 4: Still holding the yarn closet to the skein, go under the loop you just made.

Step 5: Keep holding the yarn and with your other hand pull the end of your yarn until the slip knot forms.

Step 6: Now you can pull the end closets to the skein to tighten the knot or unravel the knot. This is when you place your loop over the first nail on the loom and tighten.

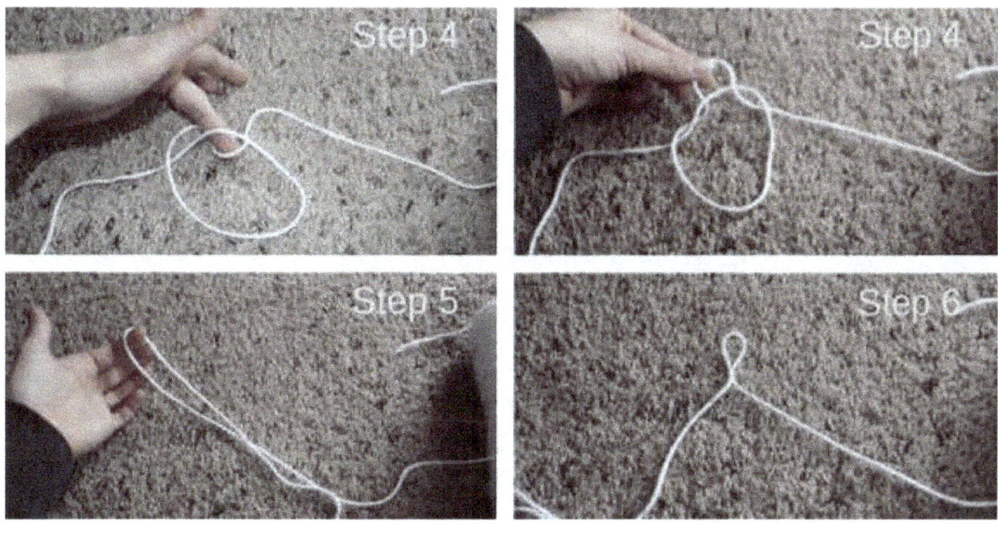

Starting your Loom

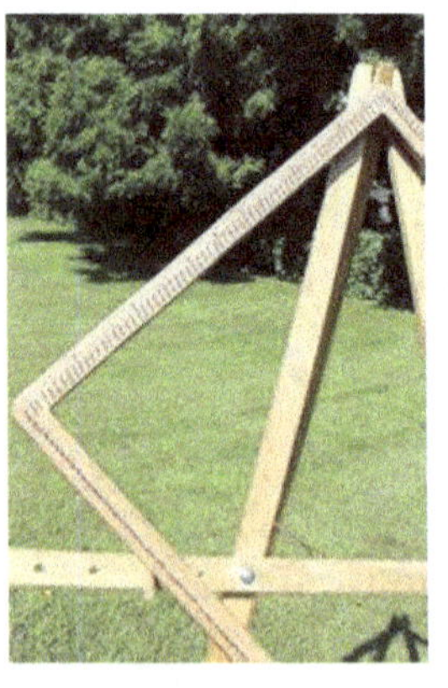

As mentioned before, I am using the first pattern, Iris Bouquet to demonstrate how to start your loom. You can find the Iris Bouquet Pattern on page 40. Feel free to use which ever pattern you'd like to try first to learn. I do recommend having extra yarn on hand, just in case.

Step 1: First get your loom in the right direction. As with all Stone Mountain Looms, the 'markings' always go to the left

*I like to wrap my first strand of yarn around the corner nail and the next nail on the bottom of the loom. This just makes it easier to weave later and will not mess up your nail count. - Ashli

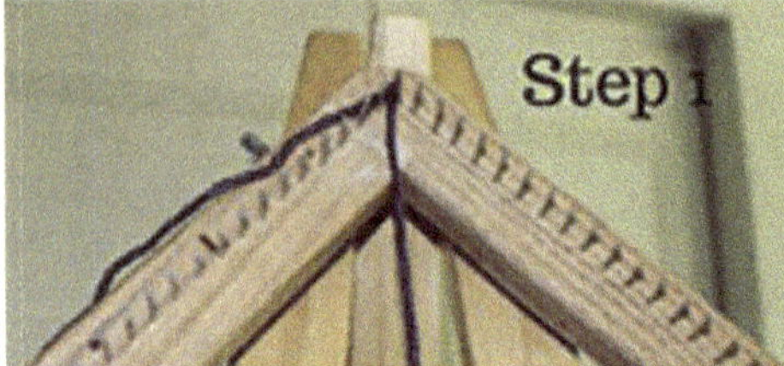

hand side on the stand. (Unless you're left handed, then you can reverse this and put the marks to the right and start in the top right hand corner). Make a slip knot and slip it over the nail on the top left hand corner of the loom.

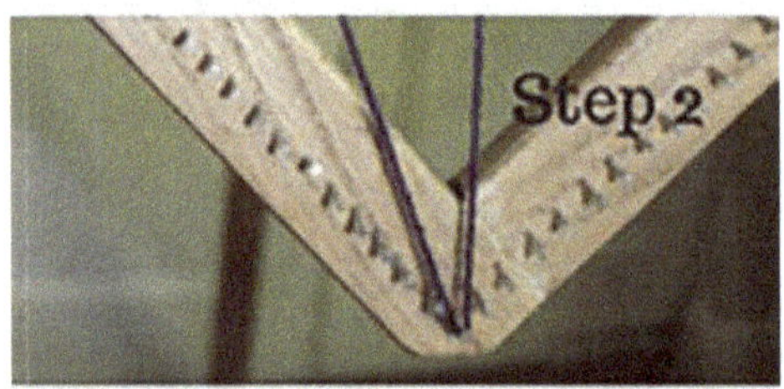

*The square loom sits more comfortably on its side. In that case, still put the markings on the left hand side. Your slip knot will go over the nail on the top point.

Step 2: Bring your working yarn (the strand attached to the ball of yarn) across the loom to the opposite corner. Bring the yarn clockwise around the corner nail.

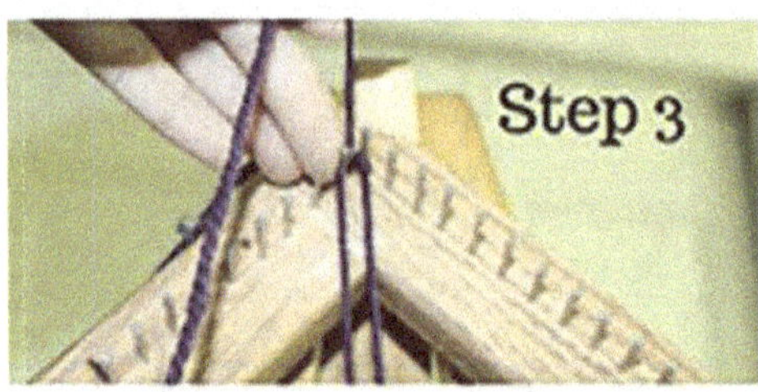

Step 3: Now bring your yarn back up to the left hand corner on the left side of your work. You're going to continue to go clockwise over the next nail on the left hand side.

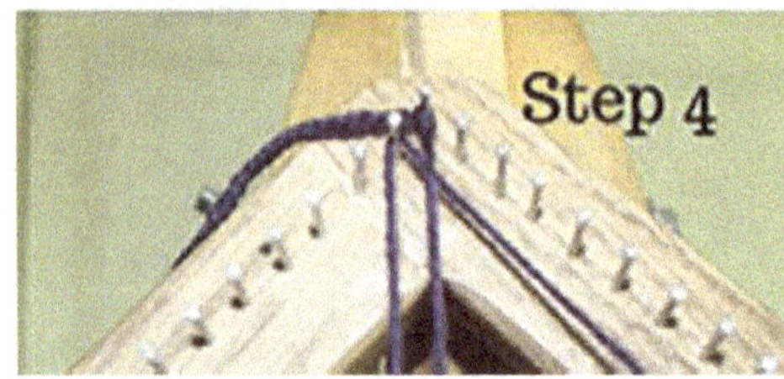

Step 4: Time to start weaving! Keeping your yarn on that second nail, carefully slide your working yarn under your first strand. Pull the yarn through, placing, still clockwise, your yarn over the next available nail on the top of your loom.

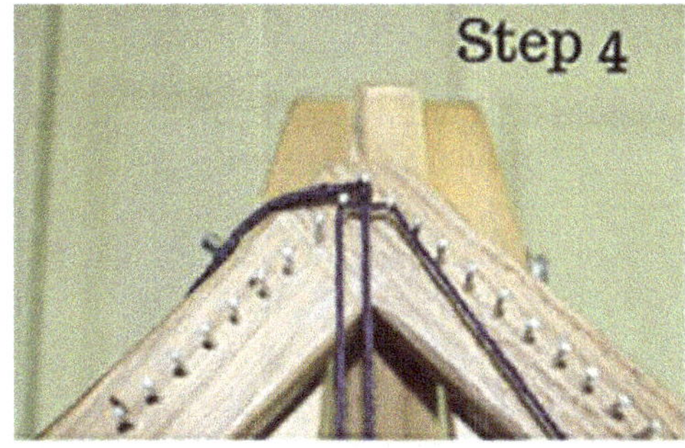

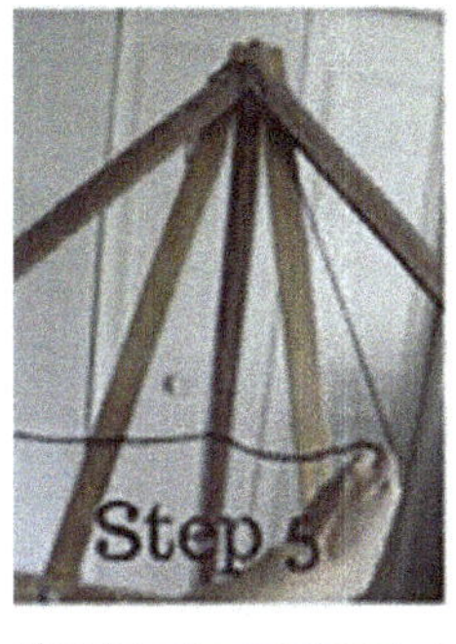

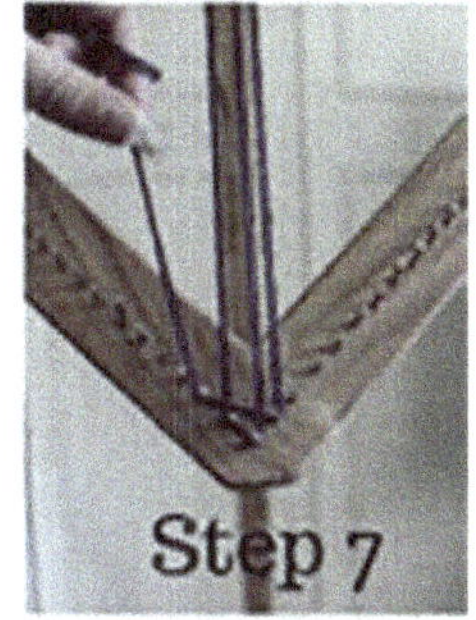

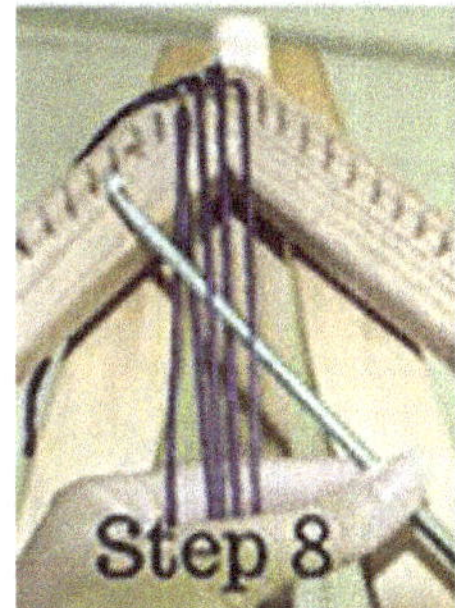

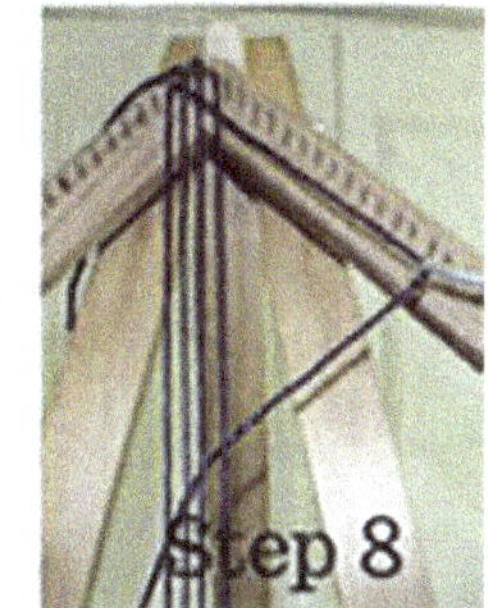

Step 5: When you wove your last strand, you actually wove two strands through at once. Find your woven part, use your right hand to hold the right side and your left hand to hold the left side of the weave. Carefully slide your weave towards the lower right hand corner.

Step 6: Using the yarn in your right hand, place it over the next available nail on the right hand side of the loom.

Step 7: Keeping the weave straight, take the yarn still in your left hand and place, clockwise, around the next available nail on the bottom of the loom.

Step 8: Bring your working yarn back up to the left hand corner and once again find the next available nail. Pick up your crochet hook and start weaving from the right. Go under then over and hook your working yarn to pull through your weave.

Repeat steps 4-8 until you're on your last row. *Please consult Page 17 on what to do when your crochet hook is 'too short'.

Finishing your Loom

Step 9: Before you weave your last row, we suggest you 'measure' your yarn. What we mean is take your working yarn and bring it from the lower left hand corner to the top right hand corner. Leaving enough room for fringe or to tie off, cut your yarn. Now you can carefully weave your last row.

*Weaving the last string can be hard to do depending on your tension. That's why we like to cut our last piece of yarn before we weave it up through the center. Bringing one string up is a lot easier to do than two.

Step 10: Before pulling your wonderful work off your loom, tie off your last strand. Then pull your slip knot off your first nail and tie off your beginning strand. Now it is ready for you to add fringe if you'd like or you can just slide it off your loom
.

*There is no need to 'bind-off' your loom. Your edges are all interwoven and will not unweave when you remove your work from the loom.

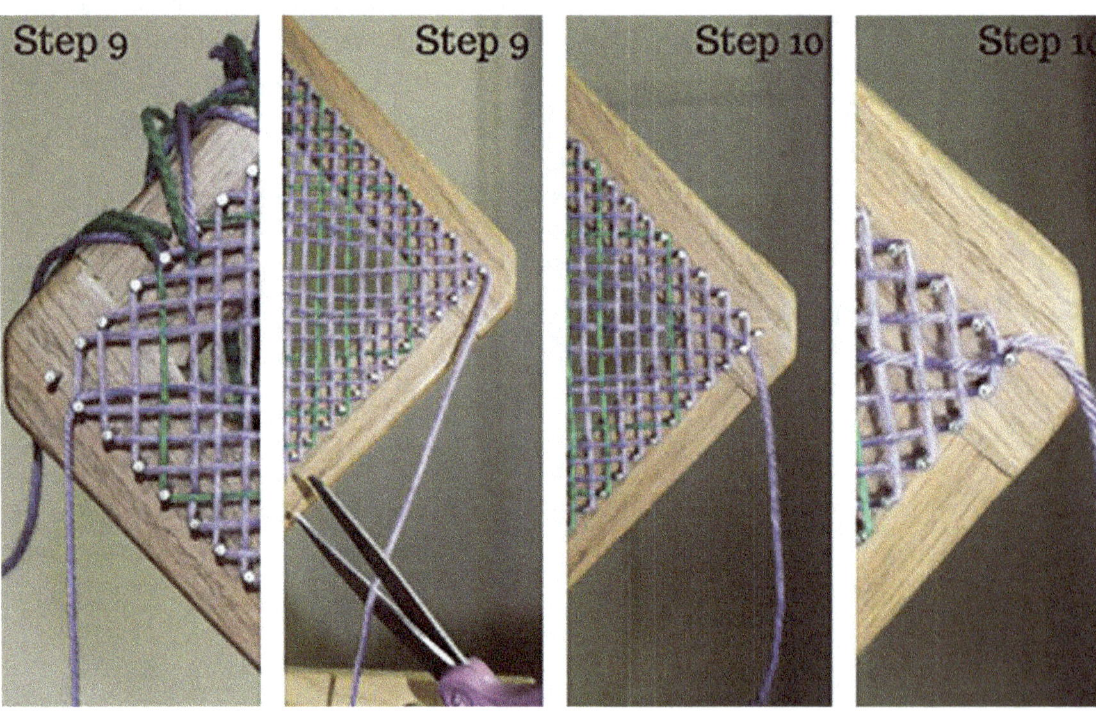

Weaving when your crochet hook is too 'short'

At some point, it will become difficult to weave your crochet hook all the way through your work. This is when you start weaving a few strands at a time, starting from the right hand side. This is hard to explain with words, here are a few pictures and steps to help you.

*Please note that the pictures were taken on a Triangle loom, but it works the same way on the square.

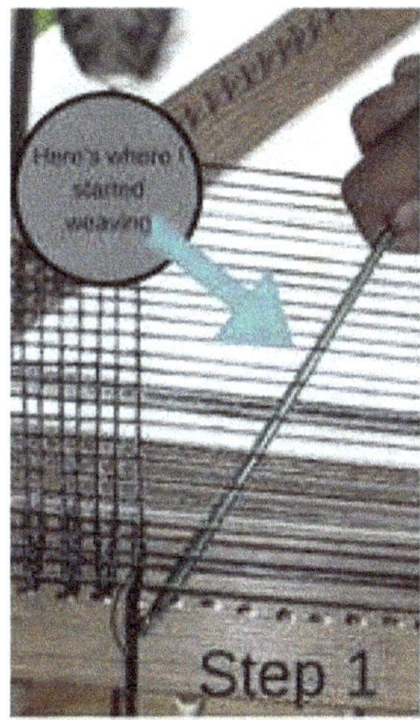

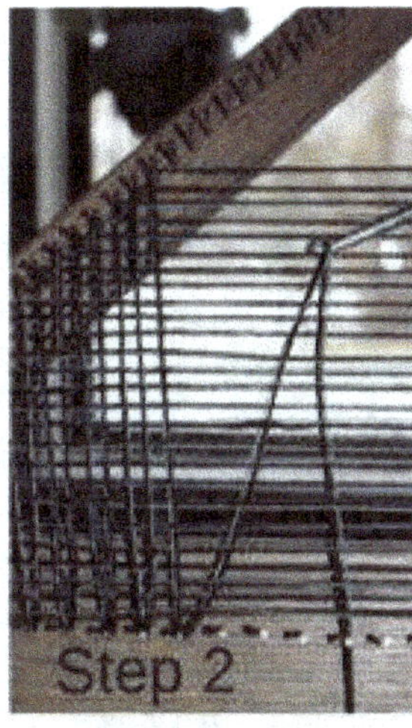

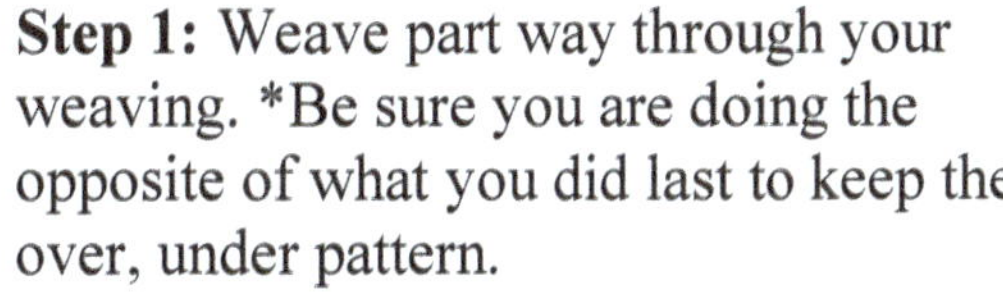

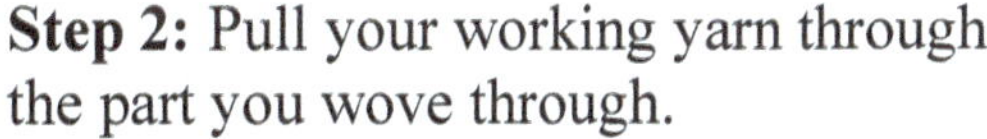

Step 1: Weave part way through your weaving. *Be sure you are doing the opposite of what you did last to keep the over, under pattern.

Step 2: Pull your working yarn through the part you wove through.

Step 3: Keep weaving part of your work, always pulling your working yarn through your work until you reach the right hand side.

Step 4: Pull your working yarn all the way to the right hand side of your work and hook on the appropriate nail.

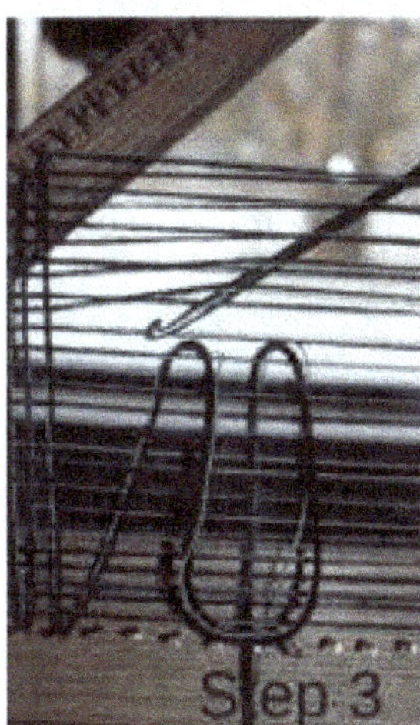

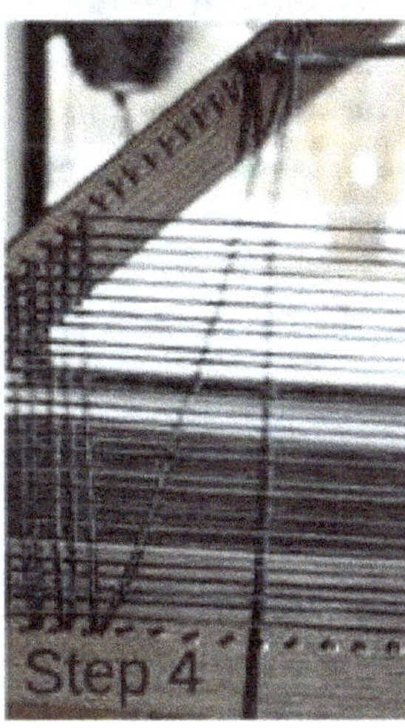

Fixing Common Mistakes

At some point in your weaving life you will find a mistake in your work. Don't worry, mistakes are easy to fix or you can leave the mistake. After all, this is a human made product. Mistakes can make your work unique.

Theresa and I make mistakes too, so don't worry. We can help you fix them! Here are the most common mistakes we come across and how to fix them.

Too Many Over's or Under's in a Row

A lot of the time you will be weaving and all of a sudden you'll realize you have three over's or under's in a row. And your pattern calls for over, under, over. You decide you want to fix it before you continue weaving.

Here's how:

Step 1: Find your mistake.

Step 2: Find your working yarn and work backwards. Slip your working yarn off the last nail you placed it on.

Step 3: Now pull on your working yarn to unweave your work.

Step 4: Keep pulling out your weaving until you reach your mistake.

Step 5: Now it's time to reweave and 'fix' your mistake. Your mistake should be fixed, and now you're ready to continue weaving your project.

Your Yarn Breaks

Sometimes while you're weaving, especially if you are working with 1 ply yarn (roving), your yarn with snap or break. You have several options before you so do not worry.

Your working yarn breaks while you are pulling it through the weaving. You can either pull out your work until you are on the left side of the loom where you can cut the broken piece off and treat it like you're changing colors. Tie the new end to the side, creating fringe and continue weaving.

A horizontal string breaks near the beginning of your work. This is scary and distressing, but we can fix it.

You can keep going as if the string is not broken and finish your work. When you go to fringe, or before you take your work off the loom, you can measure a new string to replace the broken one.

Before you pull the broken string out, here's a neat trick. You can take your new piece of yarn and tie one end to one of the broken ends. Now carefully pull the broken end with your new yarn attached through your weaving. Once you're at the end you can untie the strings, cut your broken string to fringe length and tie the new and old string together.

By attaching the two strings together and pulling them through your work you eliminate the need to re-weave a new string in the old strings place. This goes quicker than if you were to pull the broken string out and using a tapestry needle re-weave the new string in its place.

Or

Tie off your working ends. And very carefully, cut your center strings 4 at a time. Tie off the strings as fringe as you go. Once you are all the way through your work, you can now pull it off the loom.

Here's where you can get creative. If you crochet or top stitch the two pieces you just created together, depending on the size, you can make a small bag or add smaller triangle pieces to other works. Have fun with it!

Changing Color Yarn

Now that you have the weaving basics down you can get adventurous and change color!
Is changing color hard?

NO! It's not hard at all!

 It's more nerve wrecking because you're cutting your yarn which can be kind of scary.
But we are going to walk you through it.

How to Change Color:

Step 1: Get to a place where you'd like to change color, or where the pattern changes
color. Make sure you're working yarn is on the left side. The left side is where you will
ALWAYS make your changes. This applies to ALL Stone Mountain Looms and our
patterns.

Get your scissors ready. Pull some slack up where your working yarn is over the top nail
on the left side. If you're planning to leave fringe pull enough slack for the length of your
fringe.

Cut your working yarn.

Step 2: Don't panic! You did not just ruin your work, I promise. We are now ready to
change color. Pick up your new color yarn. Using your crochet hook, weave from the
right to the left of the loom, doing the opposite of what you just did on the loom. Make
sure you are pulling two strands through at once. Draw the end of your new color up
through your work and hook on the next available nail.

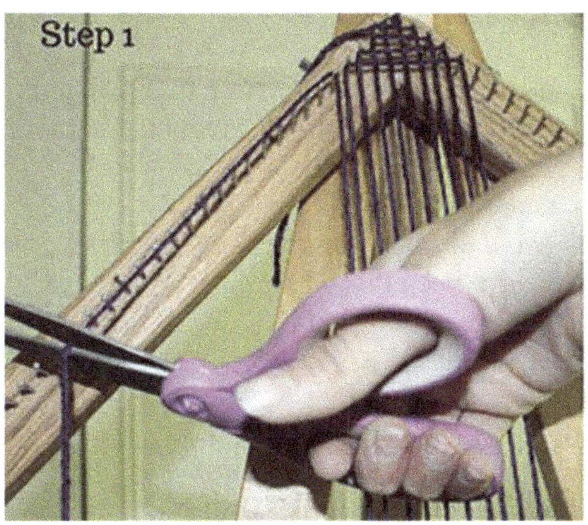

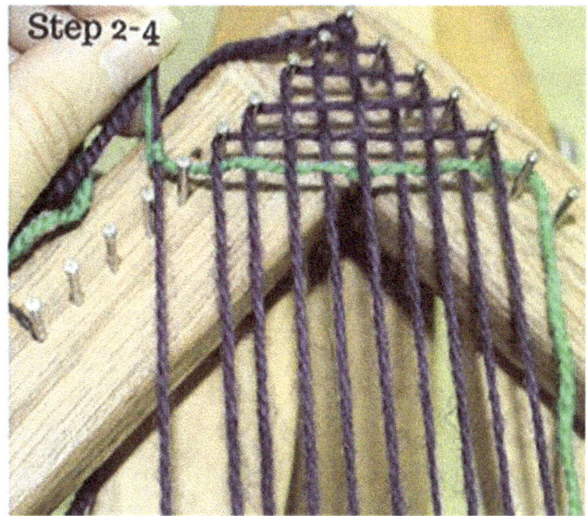

Step 3: Return to the right hand side and pull enough of your new yarn through for the length of your fringe. Use the nail you just hooked your new color on as an anchor.

Step 4: Tie your new color with your old working yarn. A simple knot will do. Just make sure it is secure and not going to loosen or slide apart as you pull on your new yarn.

Step 5: Your new color is now attached. Now you once again start weaving.

You've successfully changed colors! You can change colors as often as you'd like throughout your work. Or you can follow our patterns for two or more colors.

Happy weaving!

Adding Edges

You've just finished weaving the entire square, now what? It's time to finish your project and get it off the loom where you can add embellishments like a crocheted border, if you'd like.

We recommend when you get to the last nail on your square, you stop weaving for a minute. Yes, you have one more strand to weave through your work. You can weave two strands up through your work like you have been this whole time or you can, without weaving, bring your working yarn up to the top of your loom.

Leaving enough room for fringe, cut your working yarn.

Now you can weave the final strand up through your work.

When you get to the opposite side, it's time to tie off. You want to tie your last string to the work so it does not unweave.

You also want to tie off your slip knot. I find slipping my slip knot off the first nail before I tie it off easier than trying to pull it off after I've tied it off. You can tie off either before or after you take the slip knot off, it's up to you.

Fringe Border

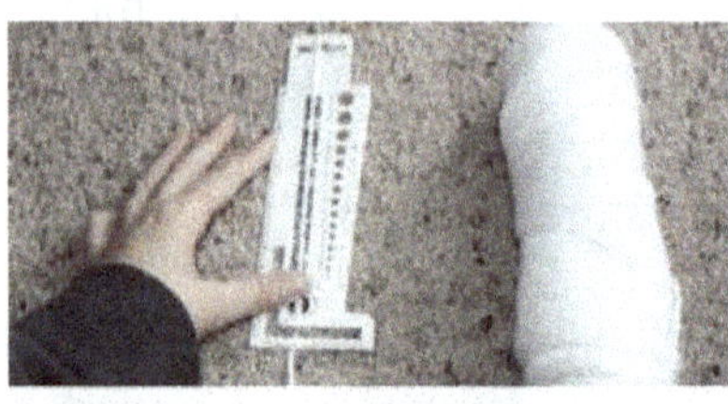

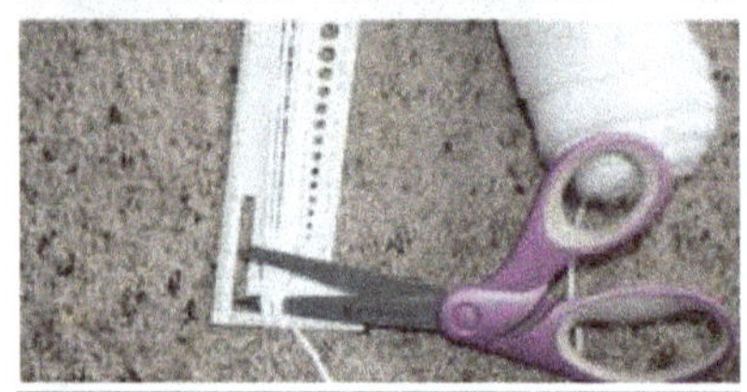

*I find a latch hook is a lot easier

Now that everything is tied off, it's time to add fringe! *If you don't want to add fringe you can skip ahead to taking your work of your loom.

Both Theresa and I use a knitting needle gauge card to help us measure our fringe (Shown left). Or, if we are in a pinch, we use our cell phones. We simply wrap our yarn around the gauge and cut it, making uniform pieces of yarn.

Using either your crochet hook or a latch hook attach your fringe to your work. We recommend you attach fringe in between every other nail. You can add as much fringe as you like. Pull one side of the fringe through your work and tie with a simple knot.

If you changed color on your work, we recommend you tie the color change ends with the fringe you're adding.

Once you have all the fringe on, you can now take your work off the loom. Just lift your woven edges up and off the nails. Be careful not to snag your yarn as you pull your work off evenly. If you do snag your yarn, it's ok. You can carefully stretch and pull the weave until your snagged piece of yarn slides back into place.

You're almost done!

Now that your work is off the loom, take a look at our Designs section and determine what you'd like to make with your finished piece!

You are finished! Congratulations! You've made something beautiful and you should be proud!

Crochet Border

You've finished your work and have decided to go with a crochet border instead of fringe. Tie off your working ends and carefully pull your work off the loom.

Theresa prefers to crochet borders after her work is off the loom. However, there are others who prefer to crochet their work as they take it off the loom. Do whichever is more comfortable for you.

Once your work is off the loom, find an appropriate size crochet hook and the yarn you'd like to use to make your border. If you've changed colors, we recommend weaving in your color changes before you start your crochet border.

There are so many different beautiful crochet borders available, we recommend you find one you like and follow the crochet instructions available.

Other Borders

Always remember the sky is the limit. There are so many other ways to finish your products, do not feel limited by the two options we have provided.

Stoney Meadows Alpacas and Stone Mountain Looms have a loom available called a flower loom. This loom creates adorable flowers that can be used in your work.

Ashli used the flower loom to embellish the border on this 3ft triangle loom shawl. You can also use the flowers to cover buttons, or shawl pins on your work.

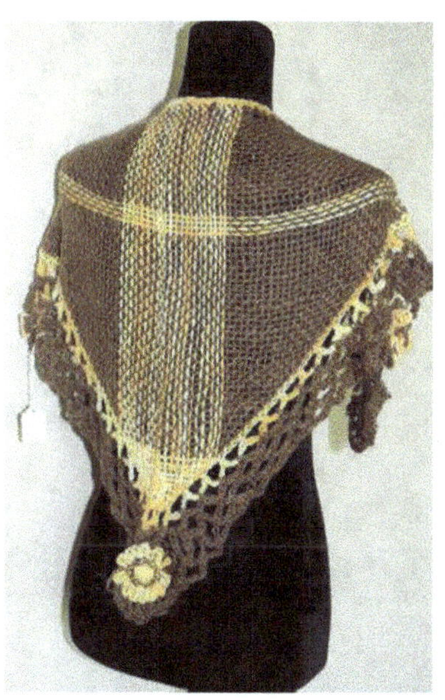

**Always remember the sky is the limit, so get creative
and have fun!

Designs

Once you are done weaving, now what? What can you do with that gorgeous piece of woven fabric? Don't worry! Here in our Design section we give a few different ways of piecing your work together to create a beautiful finished project!

Since you are weaving the same shape in this book, you can use any of the patterns in the next section with these designs. Just pick your favorite pattern and design and put them together!

*** Always, always remember, you are NOT LIMITED! Do not feel like there are no other designs you can make with this shape. Of course there are. We have just provided a few to get your creative brain a kick-start. Remember, anything you pull off the loom is a piece of fabric that you can then add to other pieces of fabric to create something bigger.

We fringed most of our designs; however, if you feel like weaving in all your ends, you can do some amazing crochet edges as well. Again, don't feel stuck in a box, break out and explore different edging techniques.

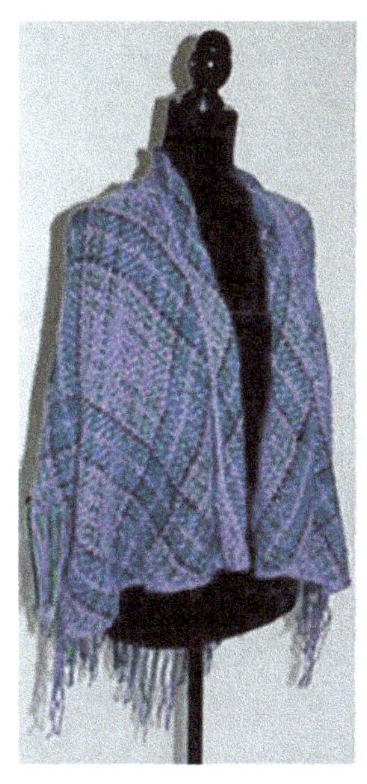
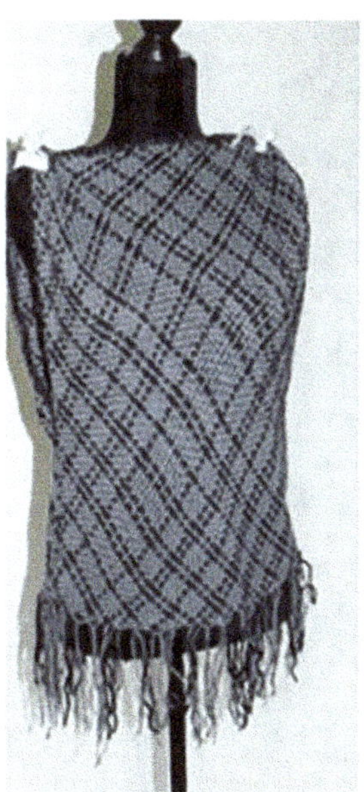
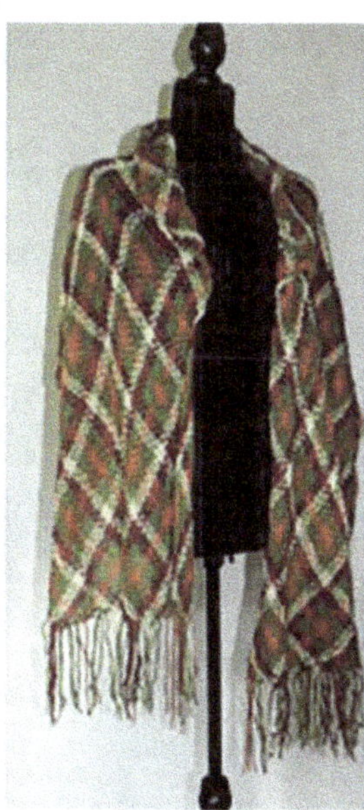
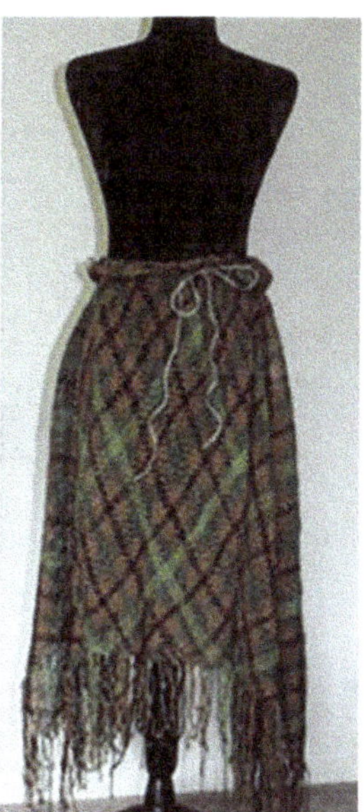

Design 1 – Wrap

Example Pattern: *Iris Bouquet*

For this design you will need to weave 3 2ft squares.

Add Fringe:

As you finish, we recommend adding fringe to your work before pulling it off the loom. Fringe can be added later, it's just easier to add it while the work is still on the loom.

On 2 of your squares, add fringe to one side only. We usually use the side we have been changing colors on, since you've already started your fringe there.

On the last square, you need to add fringe to two sides. We typically use the side you've changed colors on and the side between your starting and ending strand of yarn. We chose those two sides because the color changing side already has fringe started and the other side has your last strand, which can now be used as fringe. You can use whatever side you like, we just like these two to eliminate the need to weave in any ends later.

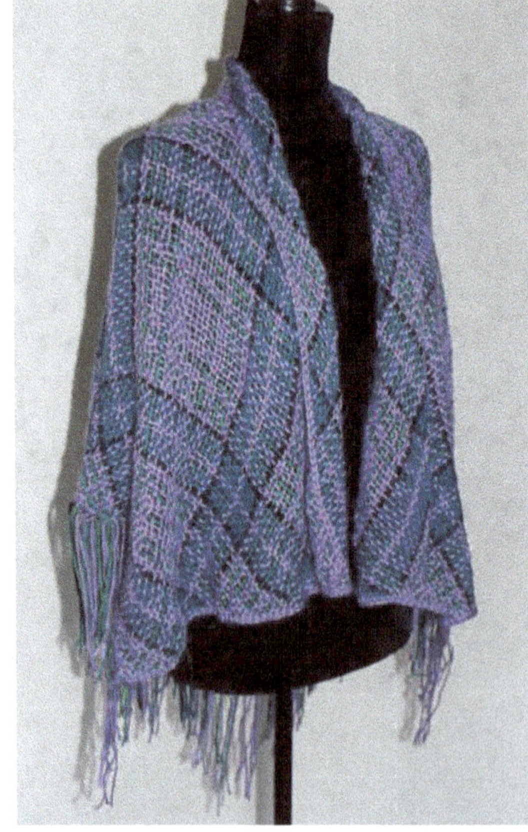

Putting together:

Now that you have your 3 squares done and fringed, it's time to put them together to form the warp shape.

The piece with two sides of fringe will go in the middle of the other two pieces. Line up your fringe so it runs along both sides, like in the picture.

We like to single chain crochet our edges together, but you do not have to. You can always sew them together using whipstitch or any method you prefer.

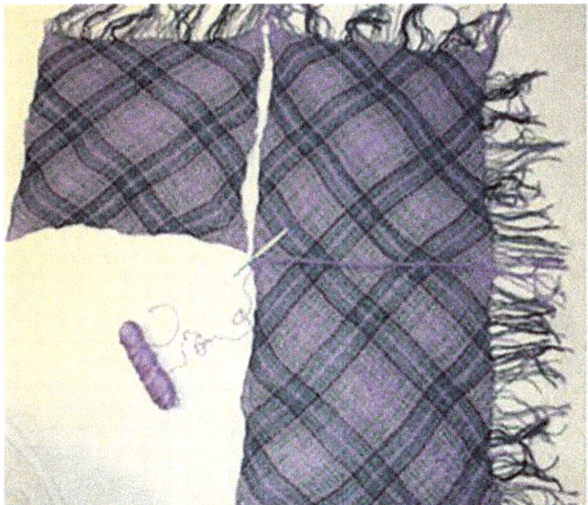
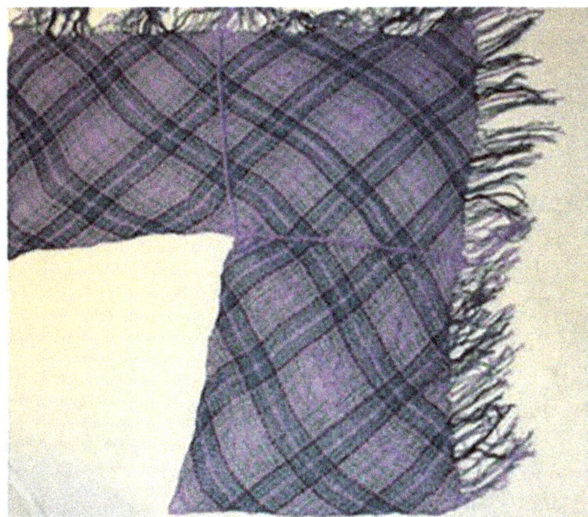

*I like to continue my single crochet around the non-fringed edge just to give my work a more finished look. Again, this is not necessary since your woven edge has a nice finish to it already.

Design 2 - Large Scarf/Wrap

Example Pattern: *Harvest Fields*

For this design you will need to weave 3 2ft squares.

Add Fringe:

      As you finish, we recommend adding fringe to your work before pulling it off the loom. Fringe can be added later, it's just easier to add it while the work is still on the loom.

      On 2 of your squares, add fringe to one side only. We usually use the side we have been changing colors on, since you've already started your fringe there.

      On the last square, there will be no fringe. Once you pull it off the loom, weave in your ends on this square.

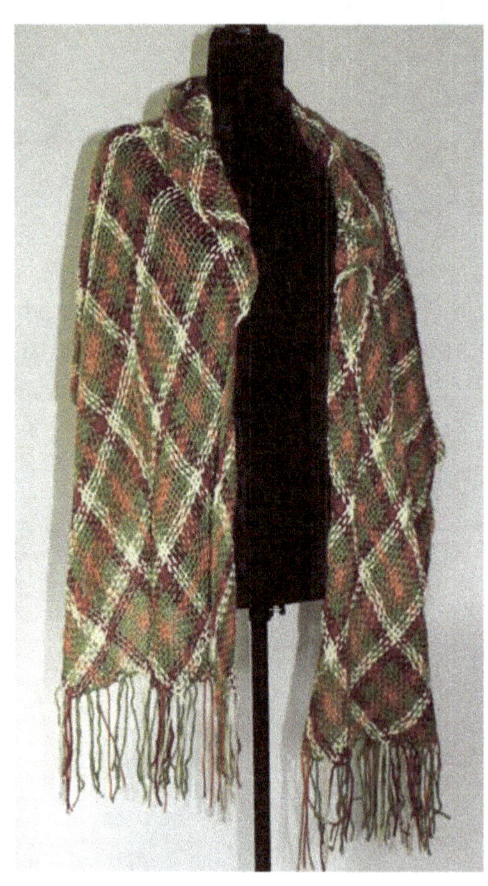

Putting together:

Now that you have your 3 squares done and fringed, it's time to put them together to form the scarf/warp shape.

Take your non-fringed piece and put it in the middle. Making a straight line, put the fringe side of your next two pieces facing away from each other on either side of the non-fringed piece.

We like to single chain crochet our edges together, but you do not have to. You can always sew them together using whipstitch or any method you prefer.

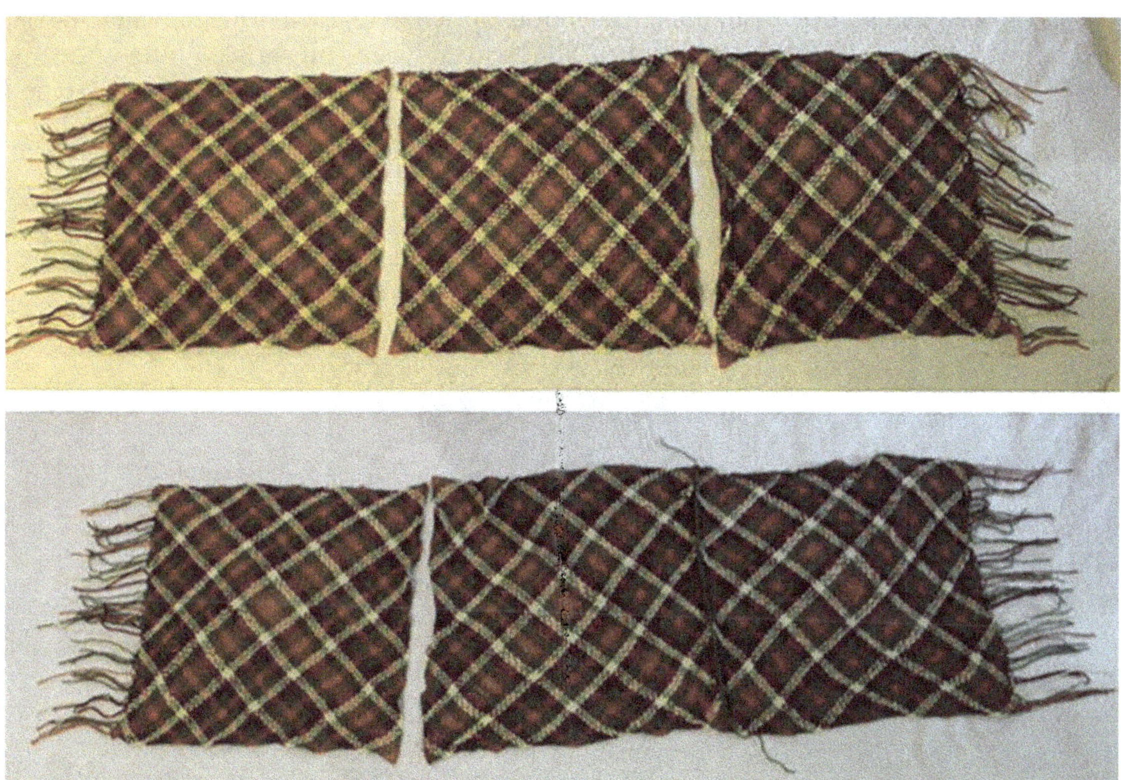

Design 3 – Bag

Example Pattern: *Autumn Splendor*

For this design you will need to weave 1 2ft square.

Add Fringe:

Fringe is optional.

You'll need a liner. I recommend a cotton fabric liner. Cut a piece to match the size of your square. (2ft x 2ft).*Remember, your woven piece will shrink a little when pulled off the loom. I found my square was approximately 22" x 22" when pulled off the loom. Sew the liner to one side of your square.

*Tip: Leave a small opening on one size to turn the two pieces inside out. This hides your sewn edges. Once turned out, you can hand sew the opening close.

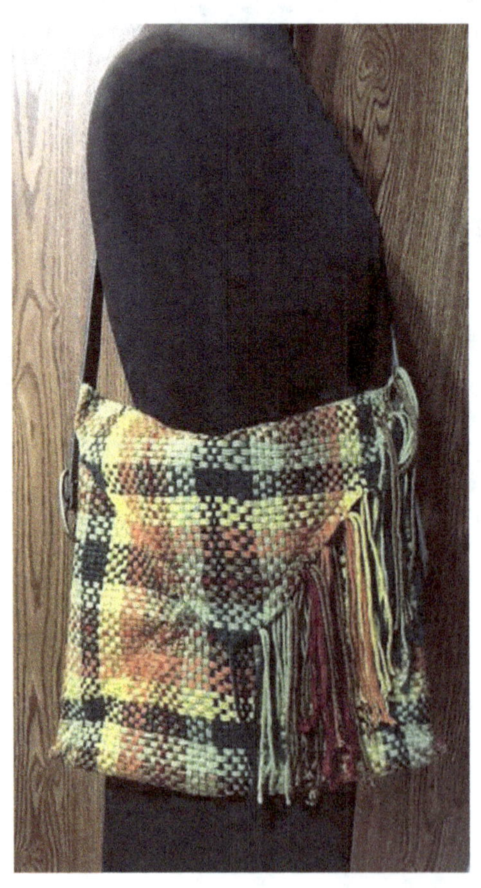

Putting together:

Now that you have your square done and lined, it's time to put it together to form the bag.

First, fold three corners to the center of your square. Sew together. The last corner is your top flap. You can leave this as is, or you can add a button.

For the handle, we choose to use a belt. Sew the two sides down on either side of your bag. Belts make great handles! They're sturdy, long lasting, and add a neat look.

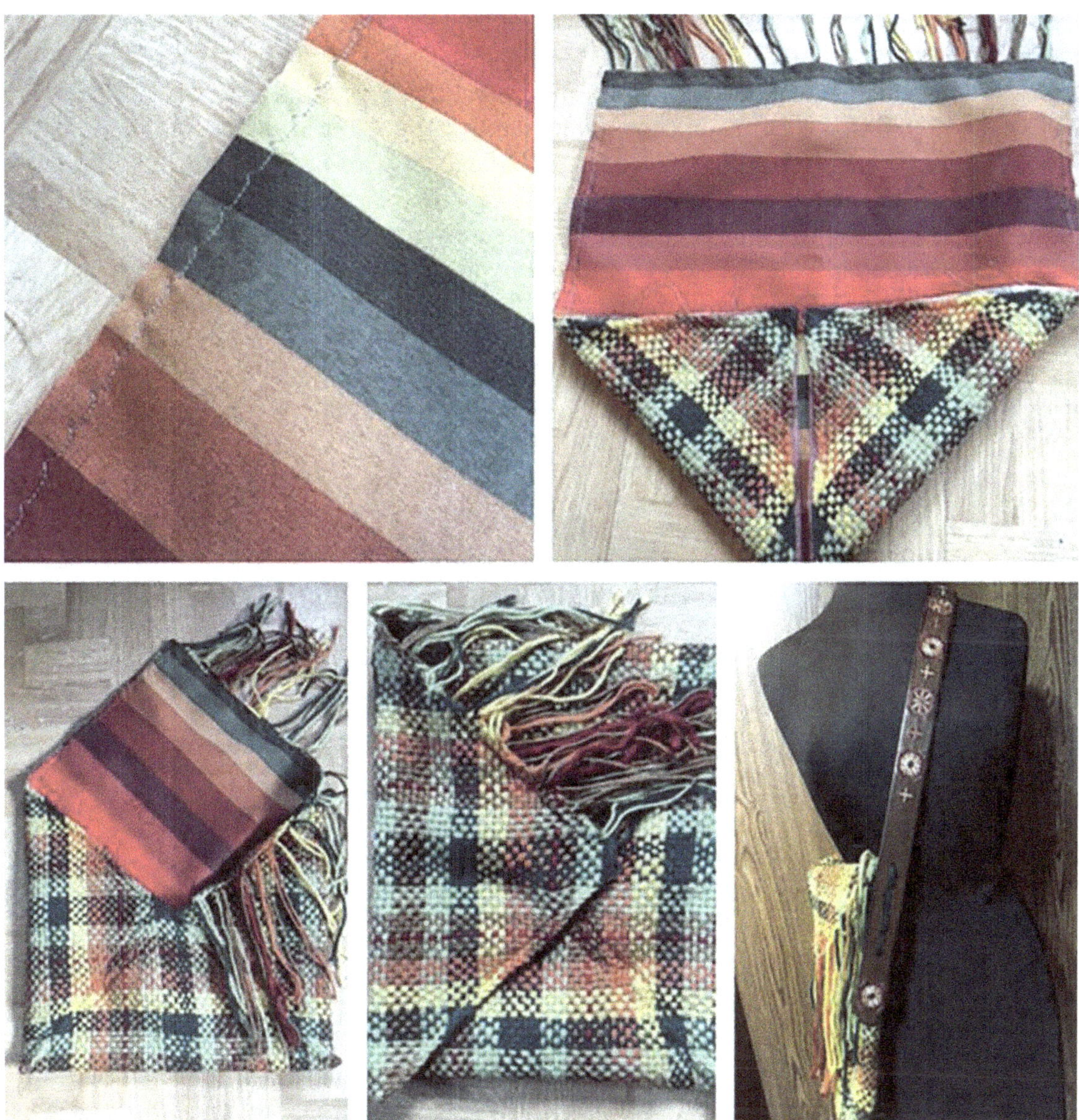

<h1 align="center">Design 4 – Skirt</h1>

Example Pattern: *Hunting Plaid*

For this design you will need to weave 4 2ft squares.

Add Fringe:

      As you finish, we recommend adding fringe to your work before pulling it off the loom. Fringe can be added later, it's just easier to add it while the work is still on the loom.

      On 2 of your squares, add fringe to one side only. We usually use the side we have been changing colors on, since you've already started your fringe there.

      On the other 2 squares, you need to add fringe to two sides. We typically use the side you've changed colors on and the side between your starting and ending strand of yarn. We chose those two sides because the color changing side already has fringe started and the other side has your last strand, which can now be used as fringe. You can use whatever side you like, we just like these two to eliminate the need to weave in any ends later.

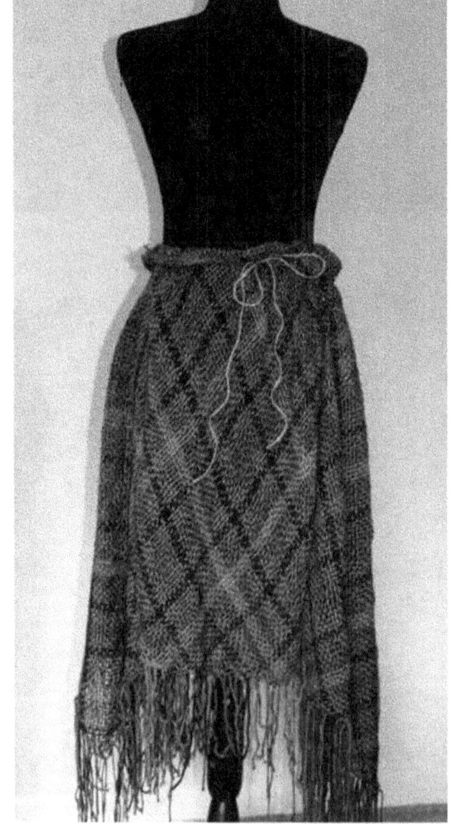

Putting together:

Weaving four squares is a lot of work, you should be proud of yourself getting to this point. Now it's time to put them together. Start by forming a wrap using 3 of your squares first.

To make the wrap:

The piece with two sides of fringe will go in the middle of the other two pieces. Line up your fringe so it runs along both sides, like in the picture. We like to single chain crochet our edges together, but you do not have to. You can always sew them together using whipstitch or any method you prefer.

Once you have three of your squares together, it is time to add that last square with two fringe sides. Lay your three squares flat. *This is to help you 'see' it better* Now lay your last piece in the same position over the other two fringed sided piece.

Next, fold your one fringed side pieces to connect to your single square. I have done this in the picture below. Just like your first three pieces, you are going to crochet/sew the touching sides together.

Once it is all together, I like to do a single crochet around the waist opening, but you do not have to. This is the fun part; find a cord to your liking. I've used jute cord, faux suede cord, shoe string, leather, and ribbon. Choose whichever suits your project best. Take the cord and weave in and out of the waist opening. I usually weave about 1-2 inches below the edge.

Once all the way around, cut your cord, and now you have a drawstring for the waist.

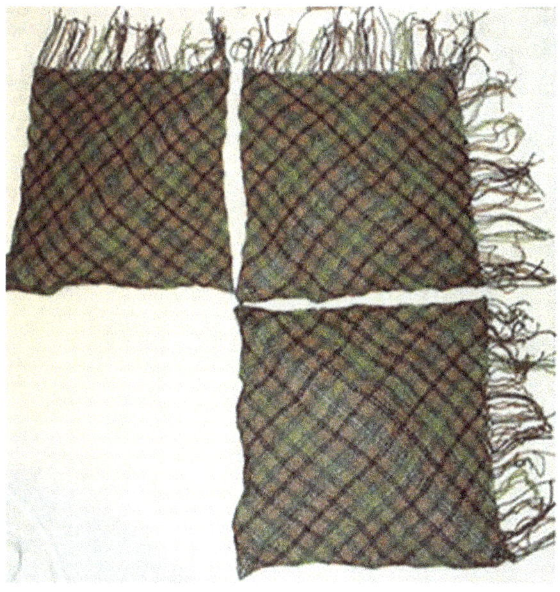
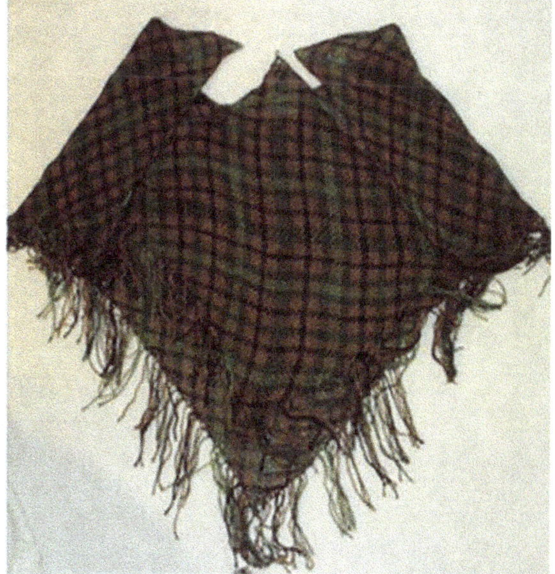

Design 5 - Shrug/Poncho

Example Pattern: *Formal Steps*

For this design you will need to weave 2 2ft squares.

Add Fringe:

As you finish, we recommend adding fringe to your work before pulling it off the loom. Fringe can be added later, it's just easier to add it while the work is still on the loom.

On both of your squares, add fringe to one side only. We usually use the side we have been changing colors on, since you've already started your fringe there.

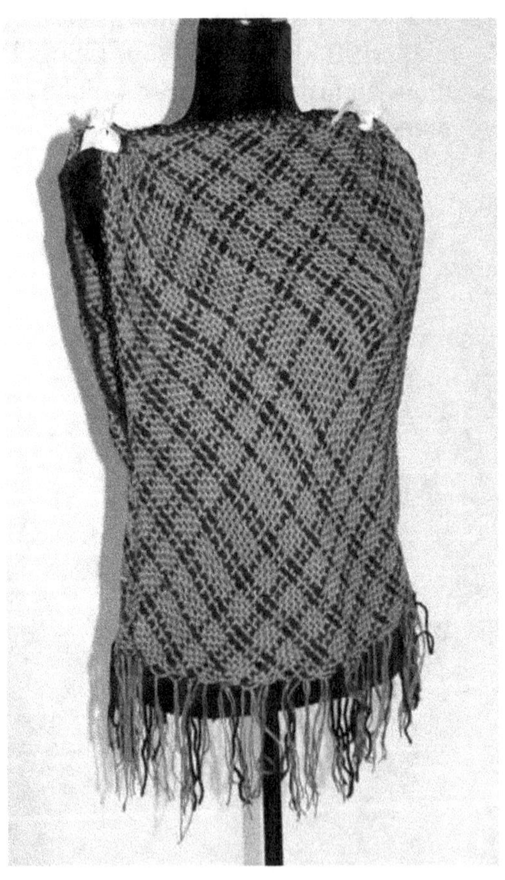

Putting together:

Now that you have both of your squares done and fringed, it's time to put them together to form the poncho. I crochet my edges together, but you can whipstitch or attach them any way you'd like.

To start, I laid my pieces one on top of the other with the fringe on the same side. Starting in a corner with fringe, crochet/sew both pieces together almost half way up the side and stop. Move to the other fringe corner, and crochet/sew both pieces together the same amount as the other side.

Now go to the opposite side of the fringe and starting in a corner, stitch the two pieces together about 2-3 inches. Repeat on the other corner. This forms your shoulder straps.

To finish, I crocheted around the neck and arm holes then found a ribbon to add a bow to each shoulder strap.

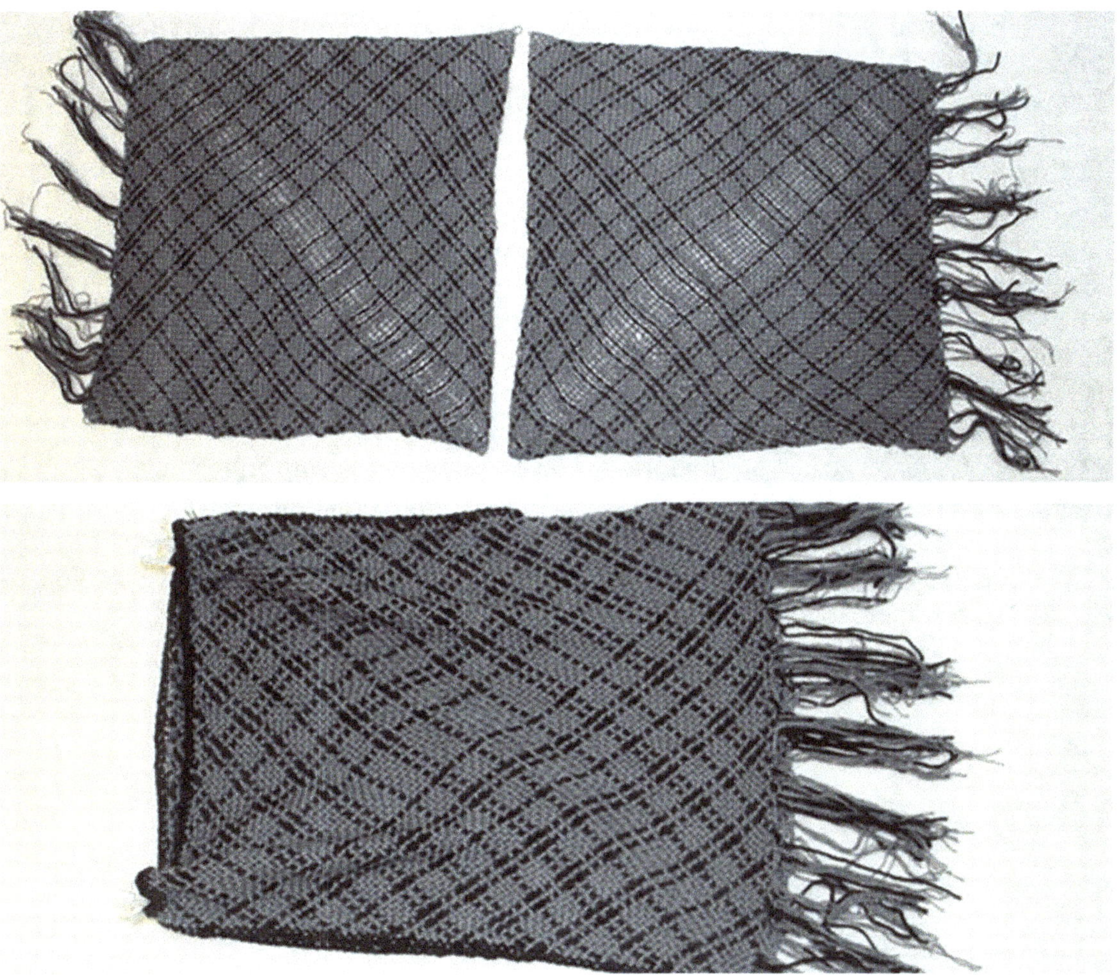

Design 6 – Blanket

For this design you will need to weave 6-9 2ft squares.

Add Fringe:

As you finish, we recommend adding fringe to your work before pulling it off the loom. Fringe can be added later, it's just easier to add it while the work is still on the loom.

On 4 of your squares, you need to add fringe to two sides. These will be your corner squares. We typically use the side you've changed colors on and the side between your starting and ending strand of yarn. We chose those two sides because the color changing side already has fringe started and the other side has your last strand, which can now be used as fringe. You can use whatever side you like, we just like these two to eliminate the need to weave in any ends later.

On 2 squares (if using 6) or 4 squares (if using 9), add fringe to one side only.

If you are using 9 squares, then there will be one square that does not get fringe. You will need to weave in all your ends. This will be your center square.

Putting together:

Now that you have all your squares done and fringed, it's time to put them together to form the blanket.

For 9 squares, put your non-fringed square in the center, your four fringed on one side pieces on each of the four sides of you non-fringed piece. The fringe should be on the opposite side that is touching the center square. Take your four fringed on two side pieces and fit them in the corners of the blanket.

For 6 squares, take your two fringed on one side pieces with fringe facing away from each other, attach the non-fringed side. Add the four corner pieces with fringe all along the outside of the blanket.

We like to single chain crochet our edges together, but you do not have to. You can always sew them together using whipstitch or any method you prefer.

Patterns

Reading Our Patterns

      To make our patterns as accessible as they can be, we have provided two different styles. The first is written out like a knitting or crochet pattern and the second is a visual chart.

      The written pattern starts on the corner nail at the top of the pattern markings. This means your slip knot. The second nail will be the nail to the left of your slip knot nail on the square. Remember you are weaving two sides at once to create a mirror image across the center nail which if you purchased a loom from Stoney Meadow Alpacas and Stone Mountain Looms, will be marked with an 'x'. The pattern is worked by putting the pattern markings on the loom on the left hand side. As you follow the pattern, you will fill in the nails from the top to the bottom.

      When you reach the center nail 'x', you will repeat the pattern backwards. Aka Nail 36 =34, 37=33, etc.

      We use all the same abbreviations as knitting or crochet patterns.

For example:
Nail 1-5: Purple
Nail 6: Green
Nail 7-9: Purple
Nail 10: Green
Nail 11: Purple
Nail 12: Green
Nail 13-14: Purple
Nail 15: Black
Nail 16-19: Blue
Nail 20: Purple

The visual chart shows all the nails from the first to the center mark on your loom. Remember, everything you do to your nails on the left will be repeated on the right.
*This is an example, not a complete pattern!

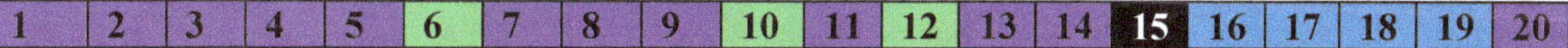

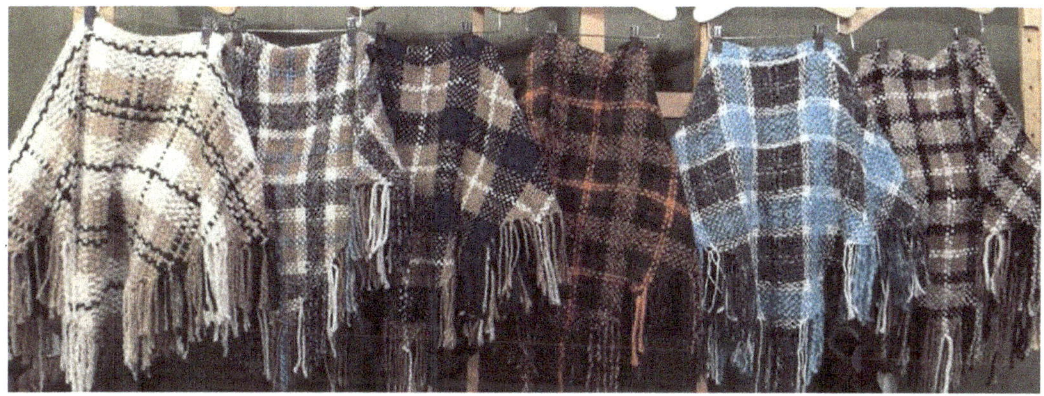

Pattern 1: Iris Bouquet

To Complete 1 Square:

Yarn – approx yardage

Purple – 80 yards
Green – 30 yards
Black – 10 yards
Blue – 20 yards

Nail 1-5: Purple
Nail 6: Green
Nail 7-9: Purple
Nail 10: Green
Nail 11: Purple
Nail 12: Green
Nail 13-14: Purple
Nail 15: Black
Nail 16-19: Blue
Nail 20-21: Purple
Nail 22-25: Blue
Nail 26: Black
Nail 27-28: Purple
Nail 29: Green
Nail 30: Purple
Nail 31: Green
Nail 32-34: Purple
Nail 35: Green

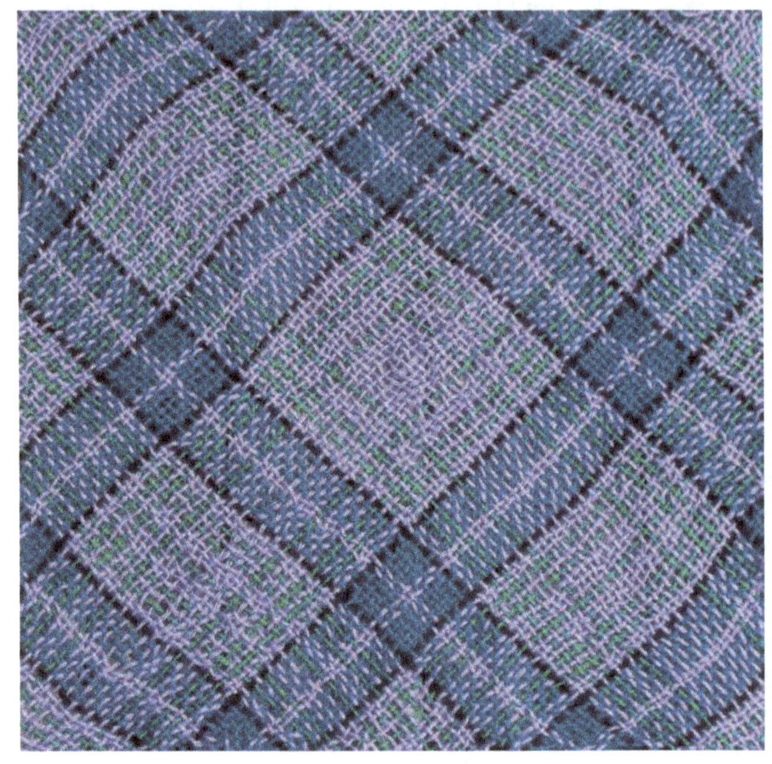

*Work the pattern backwards, starting with nail 34 as nail 36 and ending with nail 1 being nail 69.

1	2	3	4	5	6	7	8	9	10	11	12	13	14	15	16	17	18	19	20
21	22	23	24	25	26	27	28	29	30	31	32	33	34	35					

Pattern 2 - A Dusty Rose

To Complete 1 Square:

<u>Yarn – approx yardage</u>

Pink – 80 yards
White – 40 yards
Gray– 30 yards
Green – 10 yards

Nail 1-7: Pink
Nail 8-9: White
Nail: 10-12: Gray
Nail 13-14: White
Nail 15-18: Pink
Nail 19: Green
Nail 20-23: Pink
Nail 24-25: White
Nail 26-28: Gray
Nail 29-30: White
Nail 31-34: Pink
Nail 35: Green

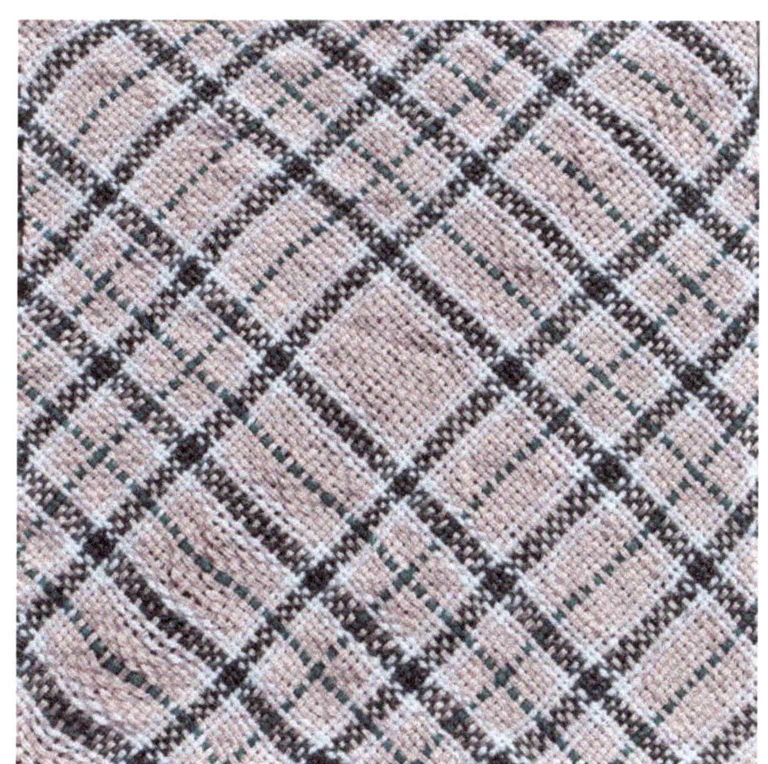

*Work the pattern backwards, starting with nail 34 as nail 36 and ending with nail 1 being nail 69.

1	2	3	4	5	6	7	8	9	10	11	12	13	14	15	16	17	18	19	20
21	22	23	24	25	26	27	28	29	30	31	32	33	34	35					

Pattern 3 - Christmas Plaid

To Complete 1 Square:

<u>Yarn – approx yardage</u>

Red – 60 yards
White – 30 yards
Green – 70 yards

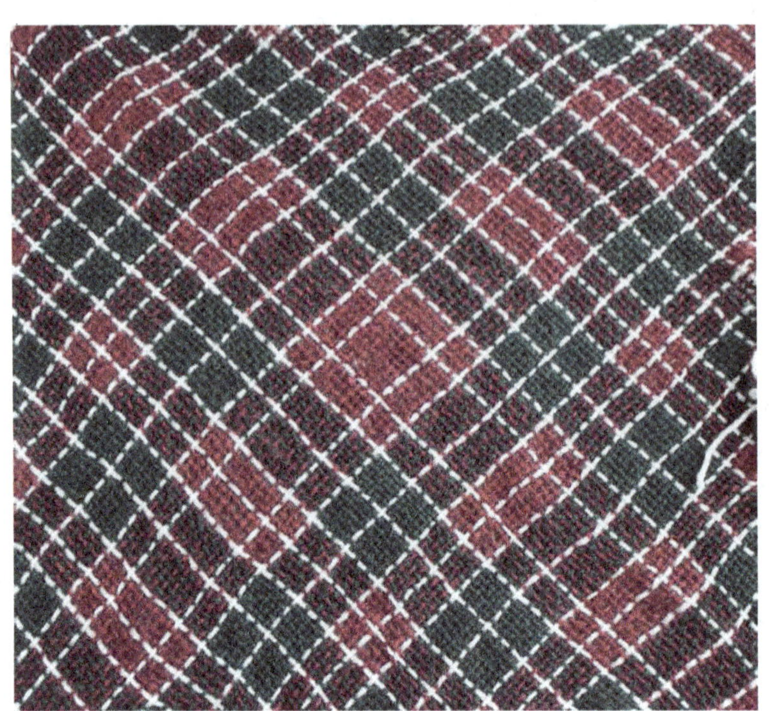

Nail 1-4: Red
Nail 5: White
Nail 6-8: Red
Nail 9: White
Nail 10-14: Green
Nail 15: White
Nail 16-20: Green
Nail 21: White
Nail 22-24: Red
Nail 25: White
Nail 26-28: Red
Nail 29: White
Nail 30-34: Green
Nail 35: White

*Work the pattern backwards, starting with nail 34 as nail 36 and ending with nail 1 being nail 69.

1	2	3	4	5	6	7	8	9	10	11	12	13	14	15	16	17	18	19	20
21	22	23	24	25	26	27	28	29	30	31	32	33	34	35					

Pattern 4 - Modern Plaid

A visually very bold plaid.

To Complete 1 Square:

<u>Yarn – approx yardage</u>

Yellow – 80 yards
Red – 20 yards
Black– 40 yards
White – 30 yards

Nail 1-3: Yellow
Nail 4: Red
Nail 5: Yellow
Nail 6: Red
Nail 7-10: Yellow
Nail 11-12: Black
Nail 13-14: White
Nail 15: Black
Nail 16-17: White
Nail 18-19: Black
Nail 20-23: Yellow
Nail 24: Red
Nail 25: Yellow
Nail 26: Red
Nail 27-30: Yellow
Nail 31-32: Black
Nail 33-34: White
Nail 35: Black

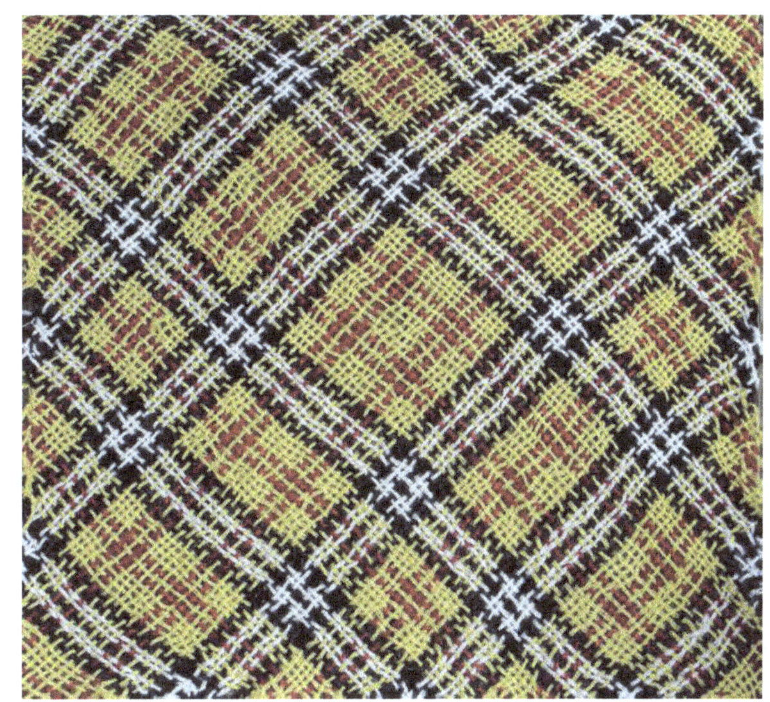

*Work the pattern backwards, starting with nail 34 as nail 36 and ending with nail 1 being nail 69.

1	2	3	4	5	6	7	8	9	10	11	12	13	14	15	16	17	18	19	20
21	22	23	24	25	26	27	28	29	30	31	32	33	34	35					

Pattern 5- Evening Sky

To Complete 1 Square:

<u>Yarn – approx yardage</u>

Gray – 90 yards
Black – 10 yards
Purple– 60 yards

Nail 1-3: Gray
Nail 4: Black
Nail 5-9: Gray
Nail 10-11: Purple
Nail 12-13: Gray
Nail 14-17: Purple
Nail 18: Gray
Nail 19-22: Purple
Nail 23-24: Gray
Nail 25-26: Purple
Nail 27-31: Gray
Nail 32: Black
Nail 33-35 Gray

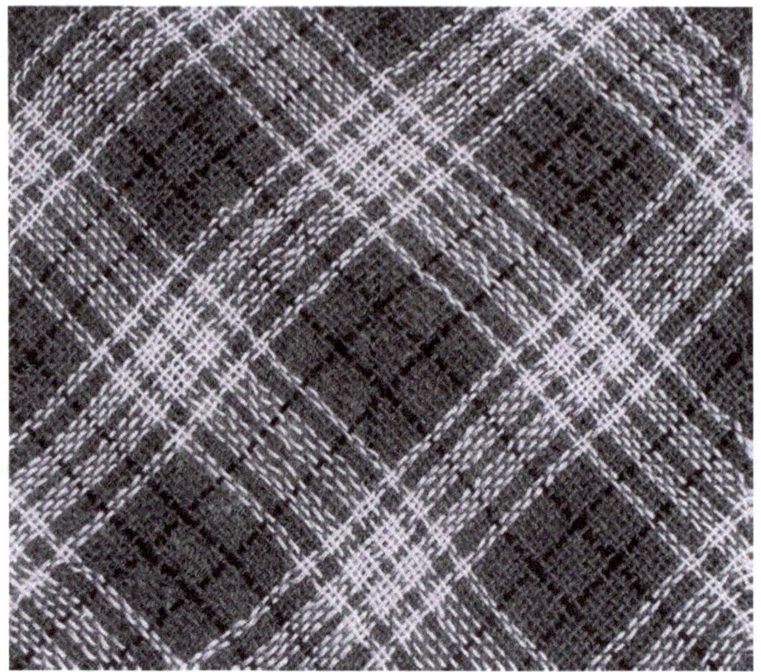

*Work the pattern backwards, starting with nail 34 as nail 36 and ending with nail 1 being nail 69.

1	2	3	4	5	6	7	8	9	10	11	12	13	14	15	16	17	18	19	20
21	22	23	24	25	26	27	28	29	30	31	32	33	34	35					

Pattern 6 - English Garden

To Complete 1 Square:

<u>Yarn – approx yardage</u>

Green – 40 yards
Pink – 90 yards
White – 30 yards

Nail 1-3: Green
Nail 4-7: Pink
Nail 8-9: White
Nail 10-13: Pink
Nail 14: Green
Nail 15-18: Pink
Nail 19-20: White
Nail 21-22: Green
Nail 23-26: Pink
Nail 27-28: Green
Nail 29-30: White
Nail 31-34: Pink
Nail 35: Green

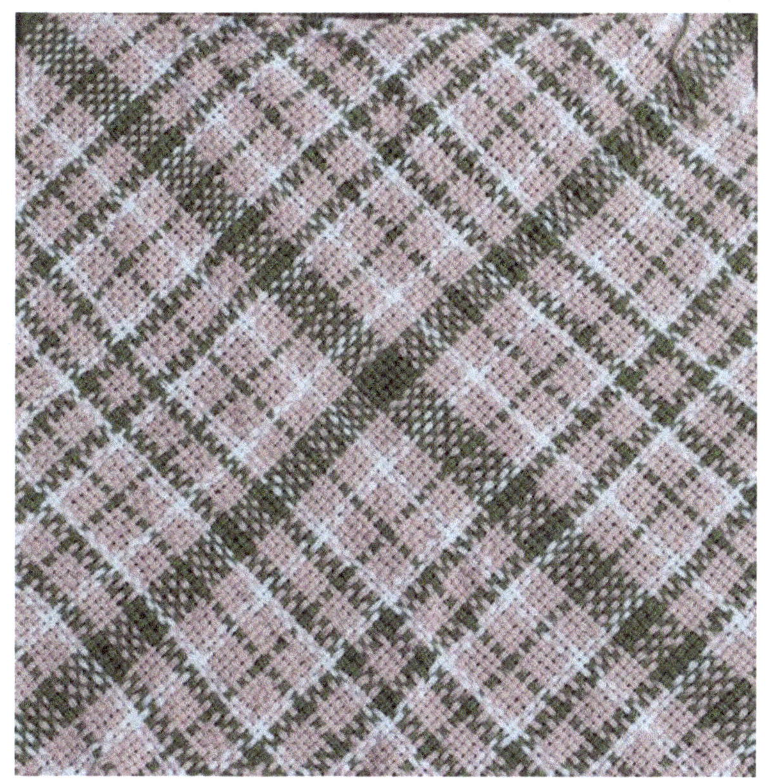

*Work the pattern backwards, starting with nail 34 as nail 36 and ending with nail 1 being nail 69.

1	2	3	4	5	6	7	8	9	10	11	12	13	14	15	16	17	18	19	20
21	22	23	24	25	26	27	28	29	30	31	32	33	34	35					

Pattern 7 - Harvest Fields

To Complete 1 Square:

<u>Yarn – approx yardage</u>

Orange – 40 yards
Green – 70 yards
Yellow – 30 yards
Red – 30 yards

Nail 1-3: Orange
Nail 4-6: Green
Nail 7-9: Yellow
Nail 10-12: Red
Nail 13-16: Green
Nail 17-19: Orange
Nail 20-23: Green
Nail 24-26: Yellow
Nail 27-29: Red
Nail 30-33: Green
Nail 34-35: Orange

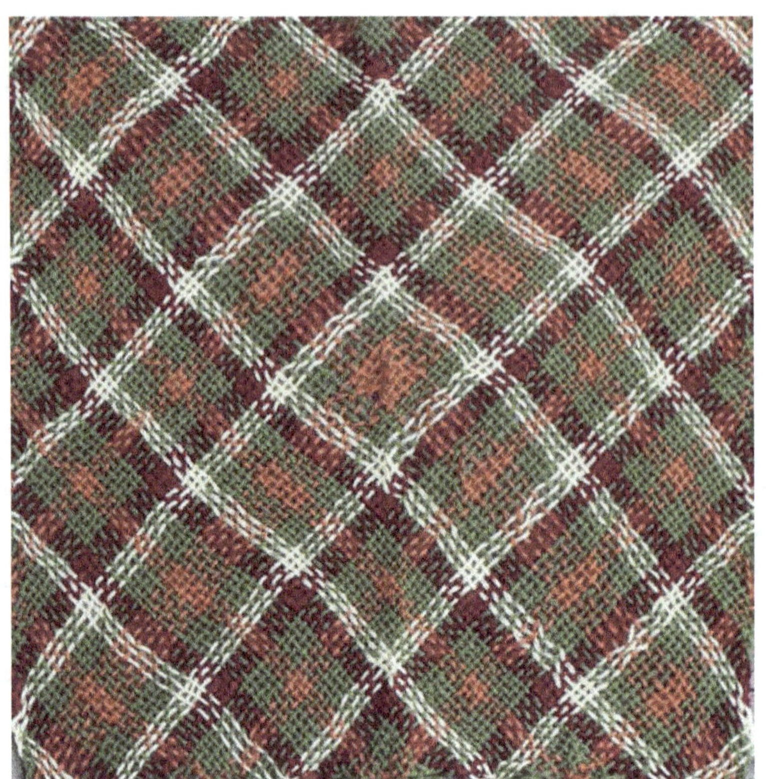

*Work the pattern backwards, starting with nail 34 as nail 36 and ending with nail 1 being nail 69.

1	2	3	4	5	6	7	8	9	10	11	12	13	14	15	16	17	18	19	20
21	22	23	24	25	26	27	28	29	30	31	32	33	34	35					

Pattern 8 - Autumn Splendor

To Complete 1 Square:

<u>Yarn – approx yardage</u>

Dark Green – 40 yards
Light Green – 40 yards
Brown– 40 yards
Red – 10 yards
Orange – 20 yards
Yellow – 20 yards

Nail 1-4: Dark Green
Nail 5-8: Light Green
Nail 9-11: Brown
Nail 12: Red
Nail 13-15: Brown
Nail 16-19: Orange
Nail 20-23: Yellow
Nail 24-28: Dark Green
Nail 29-32: Light Green
Nail 33-35: Brown

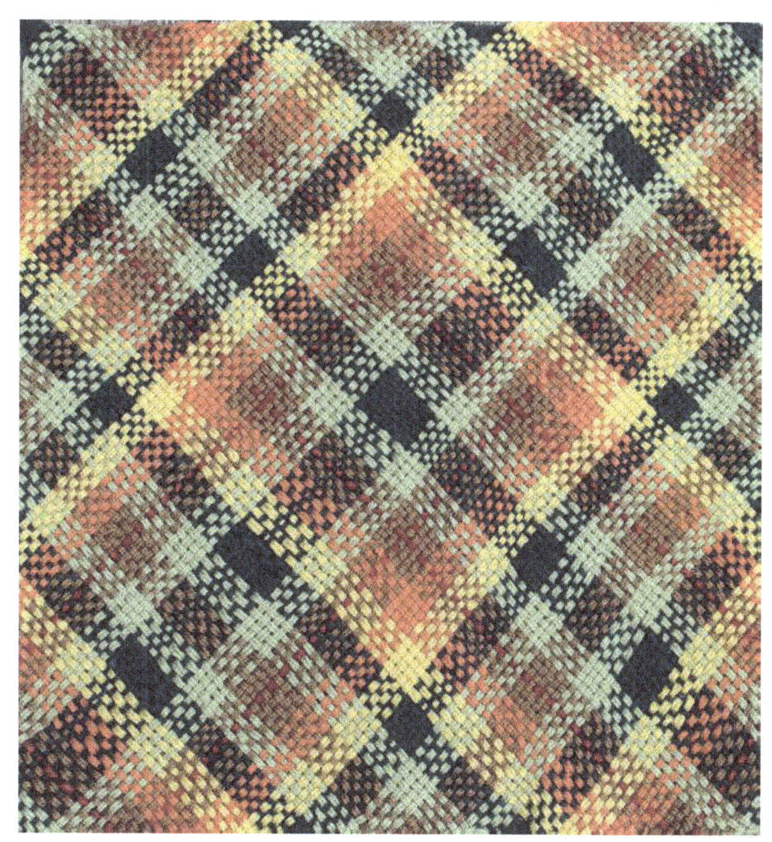

*Work the pattern backwards, starting with nail 34 as nail 36 and ending with nail 1 being nail 69.

1	2	3	4	5	6	7	8	9	10	11	12	13	14	15	16	17	18	19	20
21	22	23	24	25	26	27	28	29	30	31	32	33	34	35					

Pattern 9 - Formal Steps

To Complete 1 Square:

<u>Yarn – approx yardage</u>

Gray – 120 yards
Black – 40 yards

Nail 1-5: Gray
Nail 6: Black
Nail 7-11: Gray
Nail 12: Black
Nail 13: Gray
Nail 14: Black
Nail 15-19: Gray
Nail 20: Black
Nail 21-25: Gray
Nail 26: Black
Nail 27: Gray
Nail 28: Black
Nail 29-33: Gray
Nail 34: Black
Nail 35: Gray

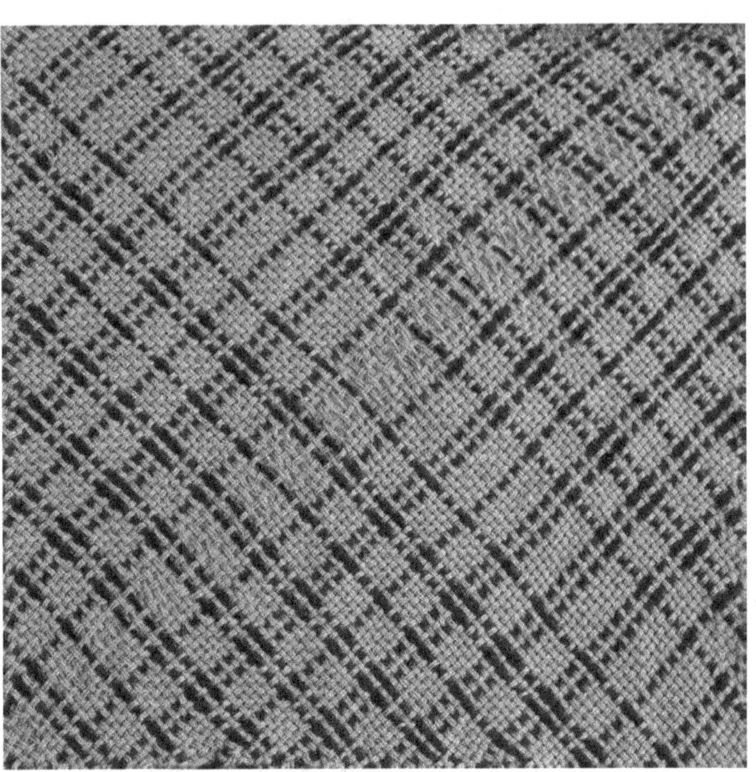

*Work the pattern backwards, starting with nail 34 as nail 36 and ending with nail 1 being nail 69.

1	2	3	4	5	6	7	8	9	10	11	12	13	14	15	16	17	18	19	20
21	22	23	24	25	26	27	28	29	30	31	32	33	34	35					

Pattern 10 - Hunting Plaid

To Complete 1 Square:

<u>Yarn – approx yardage</u>

Dark Green – 50 yards
Light Brown – 70 yards
Dark Brown– 20 yards
Light Green – 20 yards

Nail 1-3: Dark Green
Nail 4-7: Light Brown
Nail 8-9: Dark Brown
Nail 10-13: Light Brown
Nail 14-16: Dark Green
Nail 17-20: Light Green
Nail 21-23: Dark Green
Nail 24-27: Light Brown
Nail 28-29: Dark Brown
Nail 30-33: Light Brown
Nail 34-35: Dark Green

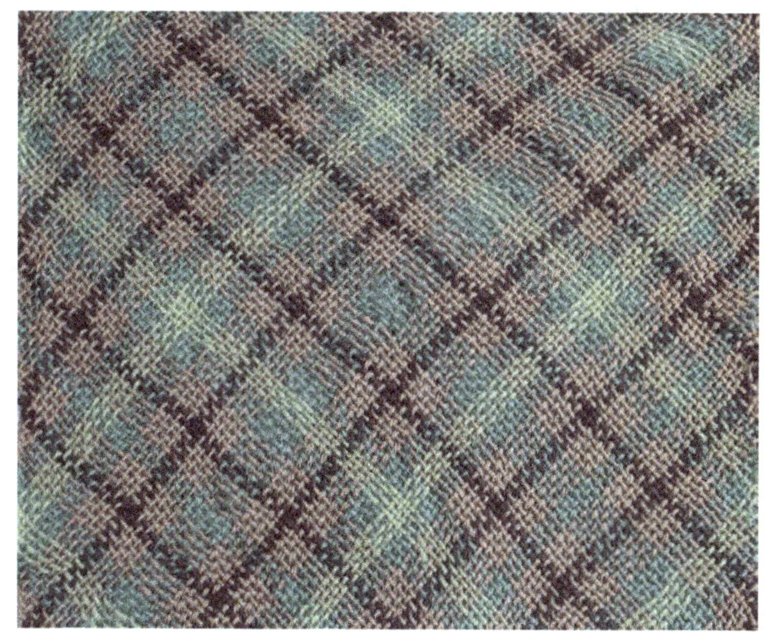

*Work the pattern backwards, starting with nail 34 as nail 36 and ending with nail 1 being nail 69.

1	2	3	4	5	6	7	8	9	10	11	12	13	14	15	16	17	18	19	20
21	22	23	24	25	26	27	28	29	30	31	32	33	34	35					

Pattern 11 - Beach Side

To Complete 1 Square:

<u>Yarn – approx yardage</u>

Brown – 80 yards
White – 20 yards
Light Blue– 60 yards
Dark Blue – 10 yards

Nail 1-7: Brown
Nail 8: White
Nail 9-13: Light Blue
Nail 14: Dark Blue
Nail 15-19: Brown
Nail 20: White
Nail 21-25: Light Blue
Nail 26: Dark Blue
Nail 27-31: Brown
Nail 32: White
Nail 33-35: Light Blue

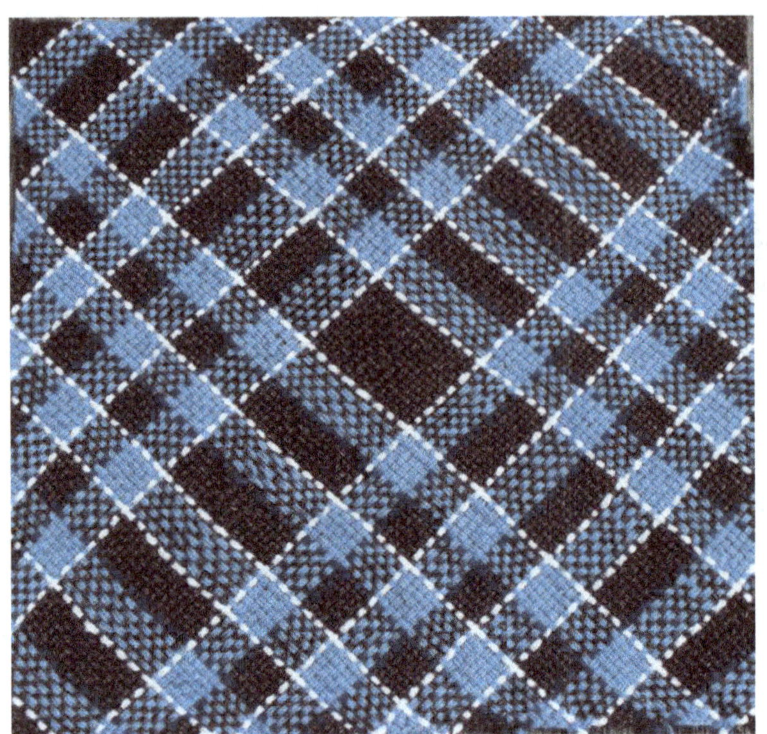

*Work the pattern backwards, starting with nail 34 as nail 36 and ending with nail 1 being nail 69.

1	2	3	4	5	6	7	8	9	10	11	12	13	14	15	16	17	18	19	20
21	22	23	24	25	26	27	28	29	30	31	32	33	34	35					

Pattern 12 - Donald

Some of our plaids are modern plaids we designs, while others are our interpretations of family plaids. We take absolutely no credit for their design, nor are they exact replicas. If you want exact family plaid patterns, I suggest getting in touch with that family.

To Complete 1 Square:

<u>Yarn – approx yardage</u>

Dark Green – 80 yards
Black – 40 yards
Blue – 30 yards
Red – 10 yards
White – 10 yards

Nail 1-6: Dark Green
Nail 7: Black
Nail 8: Dark Green
Nail 9-10: Black
Nail 11-12: Blue
Nail 13: Red
Nail 14-15: Blue
Nail 16-17: Black
Nail 18: Dark Green
Nail 19: Black
Nail 20-23: Dark Green
Nail 24: White
Nail 25-28: Dark Green
Nail 29: Black
Nail 30: Dark Green
Nail 31-32: Black
Nail 33-34: Blue
Nail 35: Red

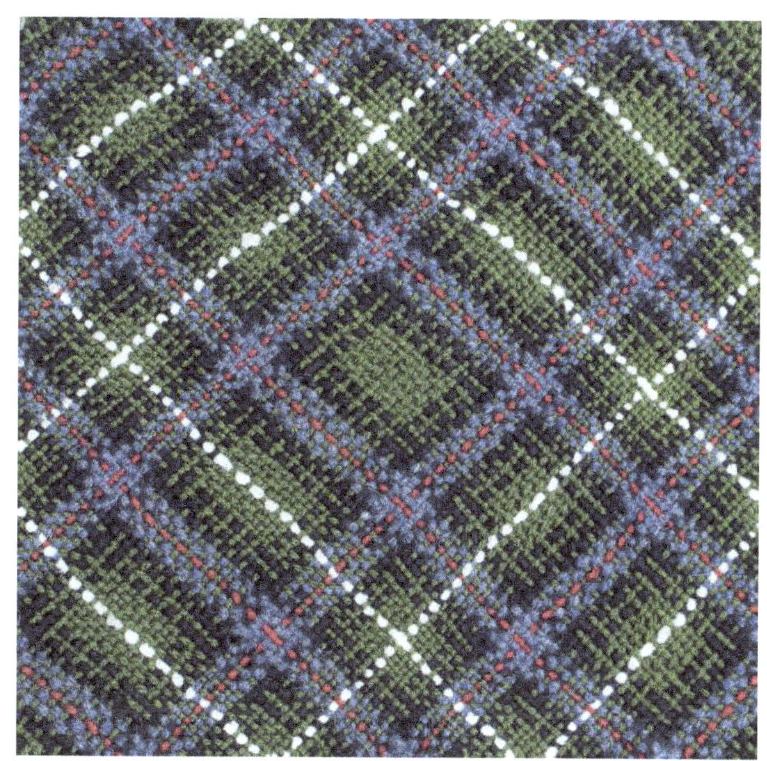

*Work the pattern backwards, starting with nail 34 as nail 36 and ending with nail 1 being nail 69.

1	2	3	4	5	6	7	8	9	10	11	12	13	14	15	16	17	18	19	20
21	22	23	24	25	26	27	28	29	30	31	32	33	34	35					

Pattern 13 - Fraser

Some of our plaids are modern plaids we designs, while others are our interpretations of family plaids. We take absolutely no credit for their design, nor are they exact replicas. If you want exact family plaid patterns, I suggest getting in touch with that family.

To Complete 1 Square:

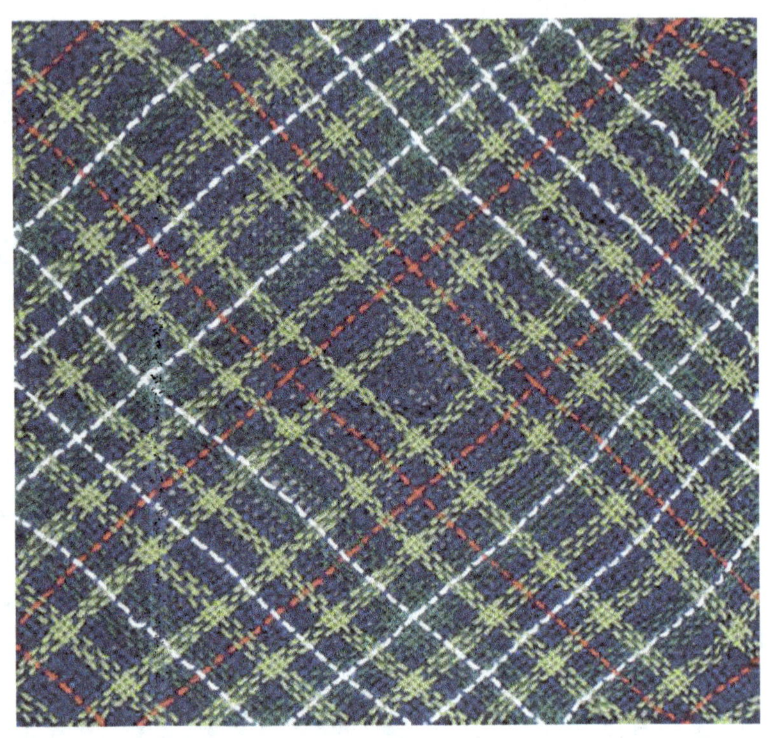

Yarn – approx yardage

Dark Blue – 80 yards
Light Green – 50 yards
Red– 10 yards
Dark Green – 30 yards
White – 10 yards

Nail 1-4: Dark Blue
Nail 5-7: Lt Green
Nail 8-10: Dark Blue
Nail 11: Red
Nail 12-14: Dark Blue
Nail 15-17: Lt Green
Nail 18-19: Dark Blue
Nail 20-22: Dark Green
Nail 23: White
Nail 24-26: Dark Green
Nail 27-28: Dark Blue
Nail 29-31: Light Green
Nail 32-34: Dark Blue
Nail 35: White

*Work the pattern backwards, starting with nail 34 as nail 36 and ending with nail 1 being nail 69.

1	2	3	4	5	6	7	8	9	10	11	12	13	14	15	16	17	18	19	20
21	22	23	24	25	26	27	28	29	30	31	32	33	34	35					

Pattern 14- Wallace

Some of our plaids are modern plaids we designs, while others are our interpretations of family plaids. We take absolutely no credit for their design, nor are they exact replicas. If you want exact family plaid patterns, I suggest getting in touch with that family.

To Complete 1 Square:

<u>Yarn – approx yardage</u>

Dark Blue – 60 yards
Light Blue – 40 yards
White– 60 yards
Green – 10 yards

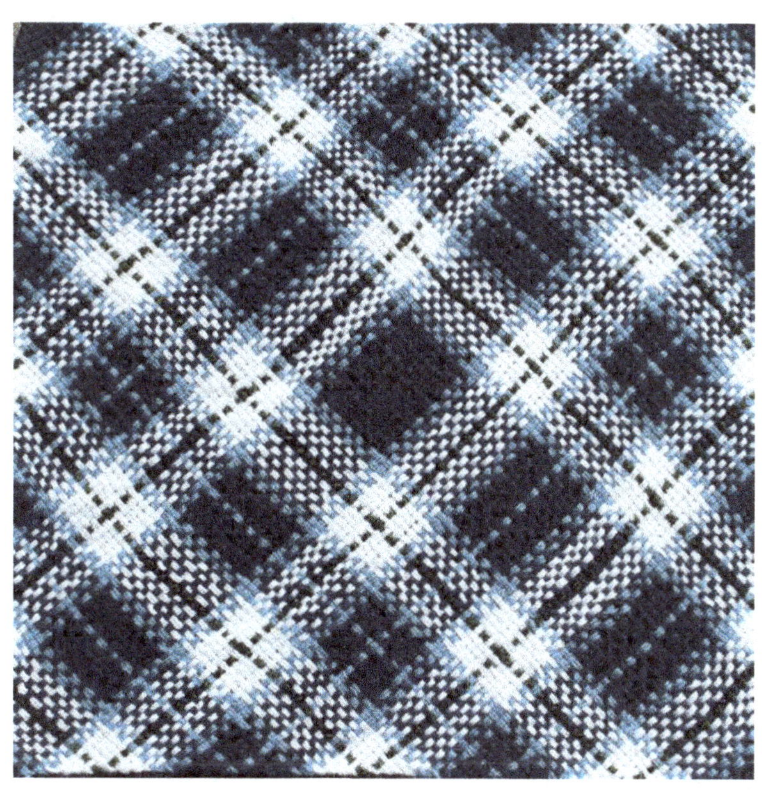

Nail 1-6: Dark Blue
Nail 7-8: Light Blue
Nail 9-12: White
Nail 13: Green
Nail 14-17: White
Nail 18-19: Light Blue
Nail 20-23: Dark Blue
Nail 24: Light Blue
Nail 25-28: Dark Blue
Nail 29-30: Light Blue
Nail 31-34: White
Nail 35: Green

*Work the pattern backwards, starting with nail 34 as nail 36 and ending with nail 1 being nail 69.

1	2	3	4	5	6	7	8	9	10	11	12	13	14	15	16	17	18	19	20
21	22	23	24	25	26	27	28	29	30	31	32	33	34	35					

Pattern 15 - Kerr

Some of our plaids are modern plaids we designs, while others are our interpretations of family plaids. We take absolutely no credit for their design, nor are they exact replicas. If you want exact family plaid patterns, I suggest getting in touch with that family.

To Complete 1 Square:

<u>Yarn – approx yardage</u>

Black – 10 yards
White – 70 yards
Light Purple– 50 yards
Sky Blue – 40 yards

Nail 1: Black
Nail 2-7: White
Nail 8-11: Sky Blue
Nail 12-13: Light Purple/Lavender
Nail 14: White
Nail 15-20: Light Purple/Lavender
Nail 21: White
Nail 22-23: Light Purple/Lavender
Nail 24-27: Sky Blue
Nail 28-34: White
Nail 35: Black

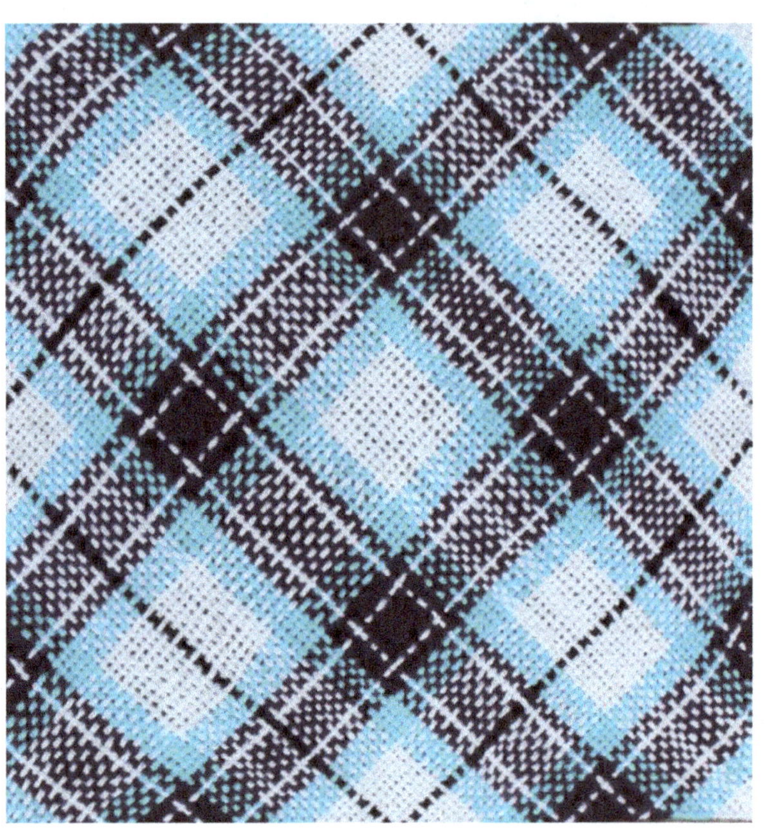

*Work the pattern backwards, starting with nail 34 as nail 36 and ending with nail 1 being nail 69.

1	2	3	4	5	6	7	8	9	10	11	12	13	14	15	16	17	18	19	20
21	22	23	24	25	26	27	28	29	30	31	32	33	34	35					

Pattern 16 - McKellar

Some of our plaids are modern plaids we designs, while others are our interpretations of family plaids. We take absolutely no credit for their design, nor are they exact replicas. If you want exact family plaid patterns, I suggest getting in touch with that family.

To Complete 1 Square:

<u>Yarn – approx yardage</u>

White – 40 yards
Black – 30 yards
Sky Blue – 30 yards
 Pumpkin Orange – 70 yards
Red – 10 Yards

Nail1-5: White
Nail 6-7: Black
Nail 8: Sky Blue
Nail 9-12: Pumpkin Orange
Nail 13: Sky Blue
Nail 14-17: Pumpkin Orange
Nail 18: Sky Blue
Nail 19-20: Black
Nail 21: White
Nail 22: Pumpkin Orange
Nail 23: White
Nail 24: Red
Nail 25: White
Nail 26: Pumpkin Orange
Nail 27: White
Nail 28-29: Black
Nail 30: Sky Blue
Nail 31-34: Pumpkin Orange
Nail 35: Sky Blue

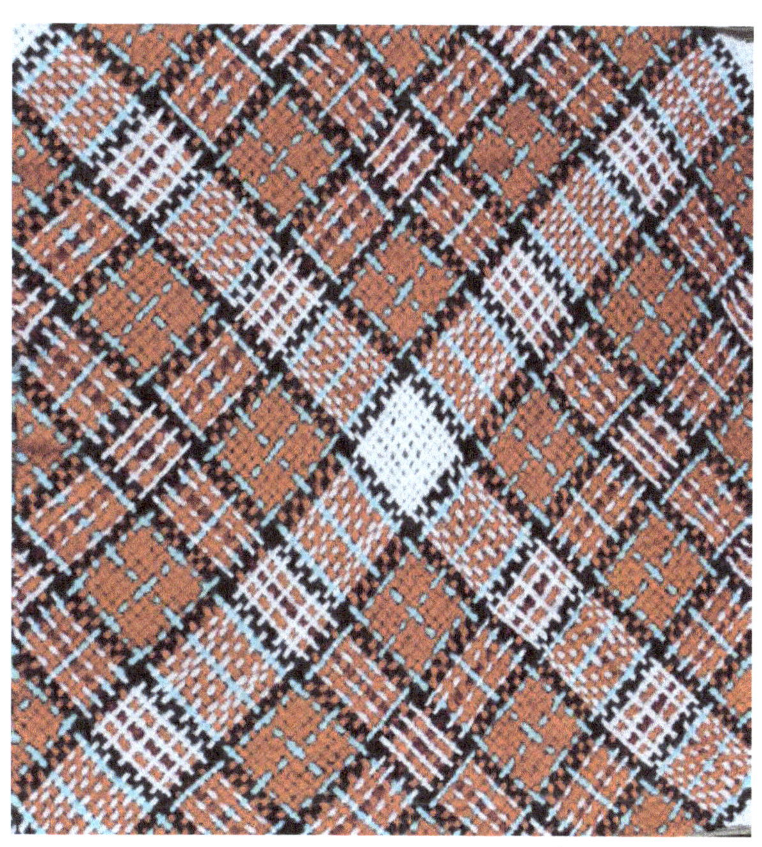

*Work the pattern backwards, starting with nail 34 as nail 36 and ending with nail 1 being nail 69.

1	2	3	4	5	6	7	8	9	10	11	12	13	14	15	16	17	18	19	20
21	22	23	24	25	26	27	28	29	30	31	32	33	34	35					

Pattern 17 - Stewart

Some of our plaids are modern plaids we designs, while others are our interpretations of family plaids. We take absolutely no credit for their design, nor are they exact replicas. If you want exact family plaid patterns, I suggest getting in touch with that family.

To Complete 1 Square:

<u>Yarn – approx yardage</u>

Red – 40 yards
Dark Green – 50 yards
White – 50 yards
Yellow – 10 yards
Dark Blue – 20 yards

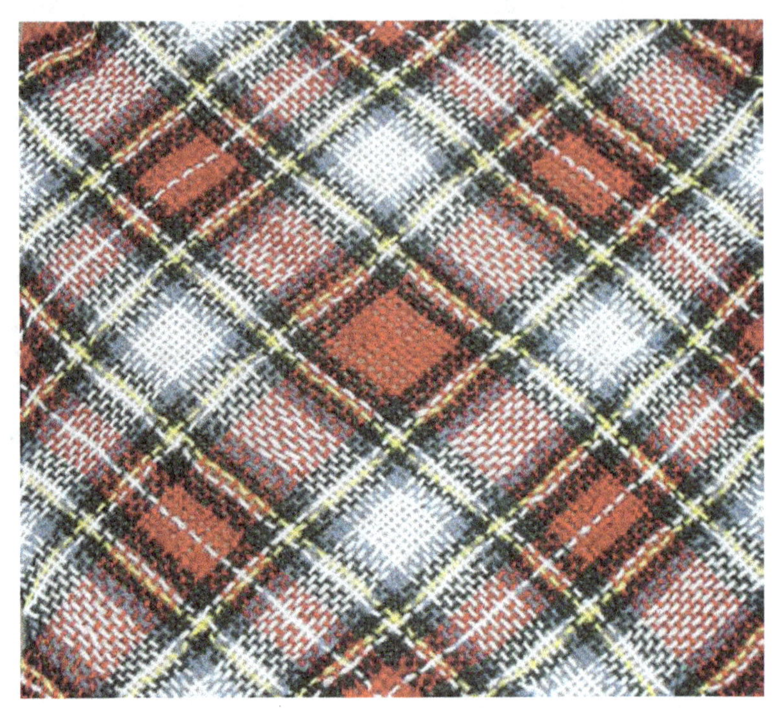

Nail 1-5: Red
Nail 6-8: Dark Green
Nail 9: White
Nail 10: Yellow
Nail 11-12: Dark Green
Nail 13-14: Dark Blue
Nail 15-22: White
Nail 23-24: Dark Blue
Nail 25-26: Dark Green
Nail 27: Yellow
Nail 28: White
Nail 29-31: Dark Green
Nail 32-34: Red
Nail 35: White

*Work the pattern backwards, starting with nail 34 as nail 36 and ending with nail 1 being nail 69.

1	2	3	4	5	6	7	8	9	10	11	12	13	14	15	16	17	18	19	20
21	22	23	24	25	26	27	28	29	30	31	32	33	34	35					

Pattern 18 - Stewart Dress

Some of our plaids are modern plaids we designs, while others are our interpretations of family plaids. We take absolutely no credit for their design, nor are they exact replicas. If you want exact family plaid patterns, I suggest getting in touch with that family.

To Complete 1 Square:

<u>Yarn – approx yardage</u>

White – 50 yards
Purple – 60 yards
Black– 10 yards
Green – 40 yards

Nail 1-3: White
Nail 4-5: Purple
Nail 6: Black
Nail 7-8: Purple
Nail 9-10: Green
Nail 11: White
Nail 12-13: Green
Nail 14-16: Purple
Nail 17-21: White
Nail 22-24: Purple
Nail 25-26: Green
Nail 27: White
Nail 28-29: Green
Nail 30-31: Purple
Nail 32: Black
Nail 33-34: Purple
Nail 35: White

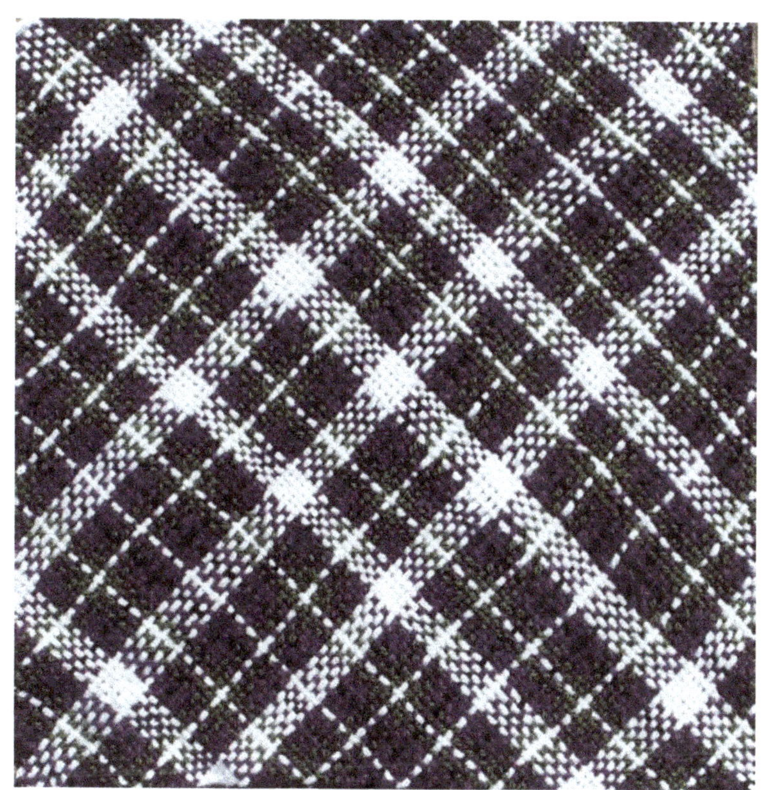

*Work the pattern backwards, starting with nail 34 as nail 36 and ending with nail 1 being nail 69.

1	2	3	4	5	6	7	8	9	10	11	12	13	14	15	16	17	18	19	20
21	22	23	24	25	26	27	28	29	30	31	32	33	34	35					

Pattern 19 - Munro

Some of our plaids are modern plaids we designs, while others are our interpretations of family plaids. We take absolutely no credit for their design, nor are they exact replicas. If you want exact family plaid patterns, I suggest getting in touch with that family.

*This plaid is worked a little differently than our other patterns. This one you do NOT repeat the pattern backwards. Follow the pattern for every nail.

To Complete 1 Square:

<u>Yarn – approx yardage</u>

Red– 80 yards
Black – 70 yards
White– 10 yards

Nail 1-6: Red
Nail 7-11: White
Nail 12-19: Black
Nail 20-24: White
Nail 25-32: Red
Nail 33-37: White
Nail 38-45: Black
Nail 46-50: White
Nail 51-58: Red
Nail 59-63: White
Nail 64-69: Black

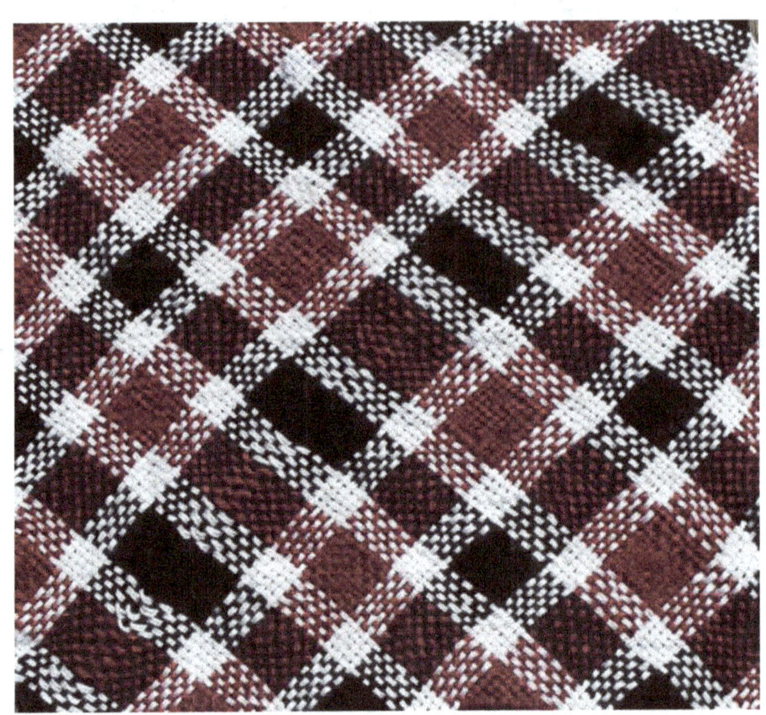

1	2	3	4	5	6	7	8	9	10	11	12	13	14	15	16	17	18	19	20
21	22	23	24	25	26	27	28	29	30	31	32	33	34	35	36	37	38	39	40
41	42	43	44	45	46	47	48	49	50	51	52	53	54	55	56	57	58	59	60
61	62	63	64	65	66	67	67	69											

Bonus Pattern/Design

Welcome to the Bonus Patterns! We have provided you with two patterns for the 6" Square loom to make adorable pouches to add to your festive outfits!

To Put Together:

First, weave 2 6" Squares on your 6" Square loom. I left the fringe on the bottom since there was a lot to weave in. But you can weave them in if you'd like.

Laying them flat together, whip-stitch/sew three of the sides together. *Tuck the fringe on the inside and sew around, then flip it inside out to make it easier to sew and have the fringe on the outside.*

Get a cord and weave about 1-2 inches from the opening to create the tie to close your pouch. Your done!

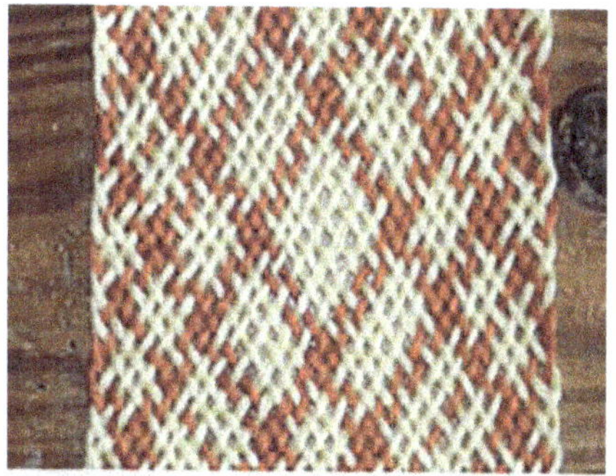

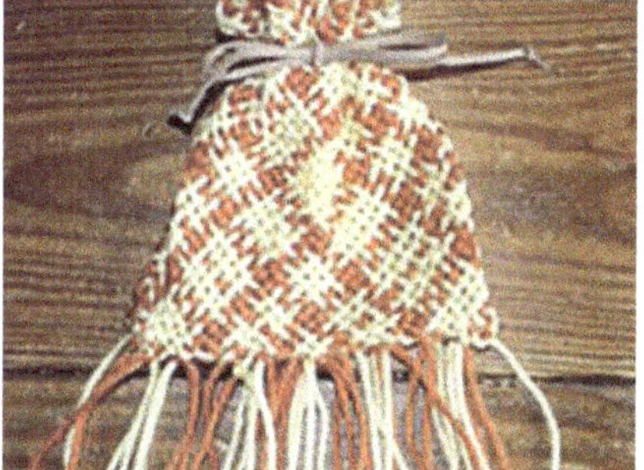

Pattern 1:

Nail 1-3: Yellow
Nail 4-5: Orange
Nail 6-8: Yellow
Nail 9-10: Orange
Nail 11-12: Yellow
Nail 13: Orange

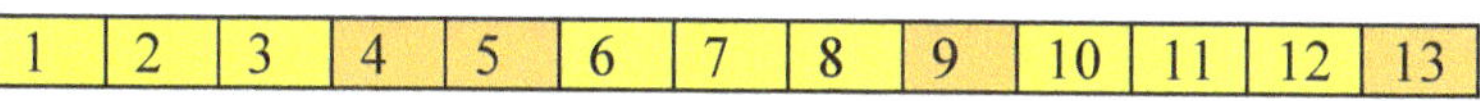

1	2	3	4	5	6	7	8	9	10	11	12	13

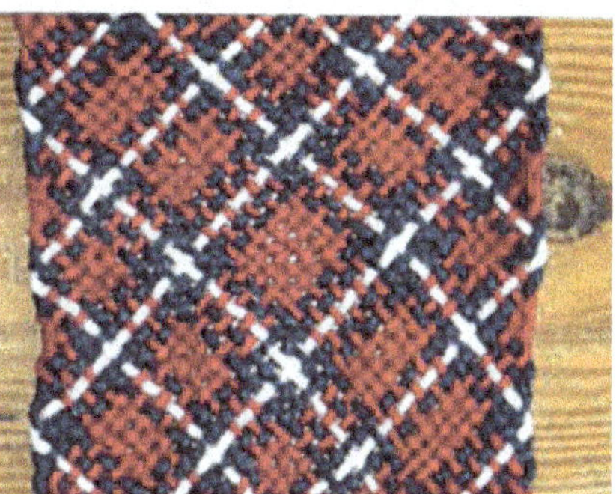

Pattern 2:

Nail 1-3: Red
Nail 4-5: Blue
Nail 6: White
Nail 7-8: Blue
Nail 9-11: Red
Nail 12: Blue
Nail 13: White

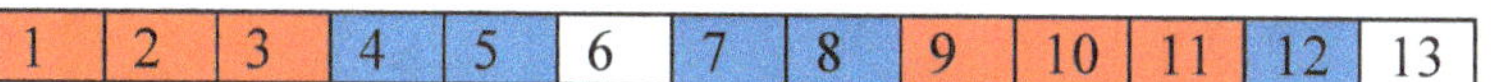

1	2	3	4	5	6	7	8	9	10	11	12	13

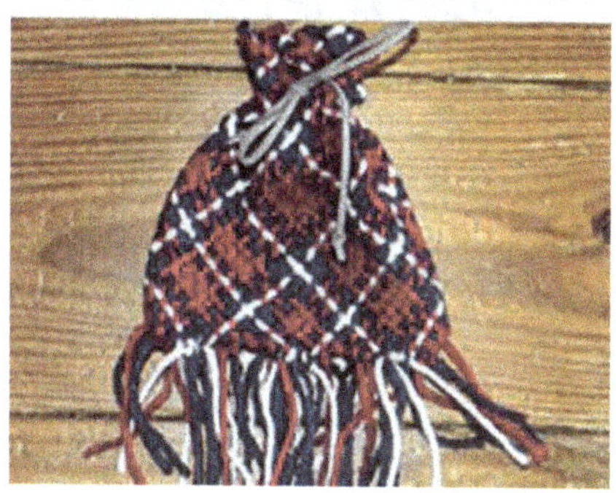

Reference

Looms and Yardage

*The yardage calculated is only for the loom and a simple border including fringe. Any other more complex border or embellishments will require more yardage. I have rounded my approximate yards up to make sure you have enough to finish your project. Our main goal is you buy enough yarn to complete your project with some left over.

Triangle Looms
6ft Triangle – approx. 600 yards
5ft Triangle – approx. 500 yards
4ft Triangle – approx. 400 yards
3ft Triangle – approx. 300 yards
2ft Triangle – approx. 200 yards
18in Triangle – approx. 150 yards
12in Triangle – approx. 100 yards

Rectangle Looms
21x63in Mobius Rectangle Loom – approx. 500 yards
10x60in Rectangle loom 10x60 – approx. 250 yards

Square Looms
6in x 6in Square – approx. 50 yards
12in x 12in Square – approx. 150 yards
2ft x 2ft Square – approx. 250 yards
3ft x 3ft Rug Square –approx. 600 yards

Diamond Looms
12in x 12in Diamond – approx. 150 yards
2ft x 2ft Diamond – approx. 250 yards

Flower Loom

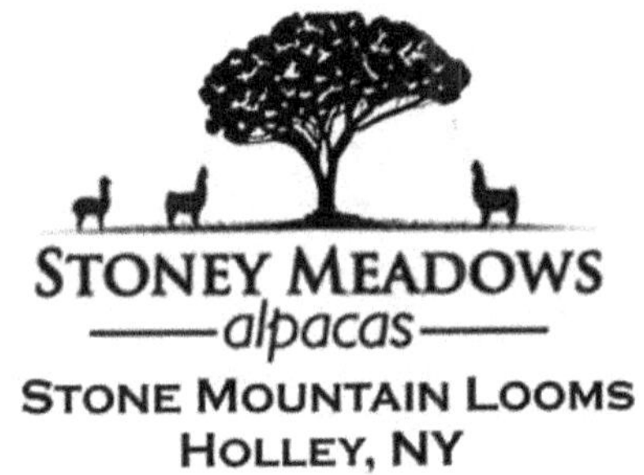

Meet the Authors

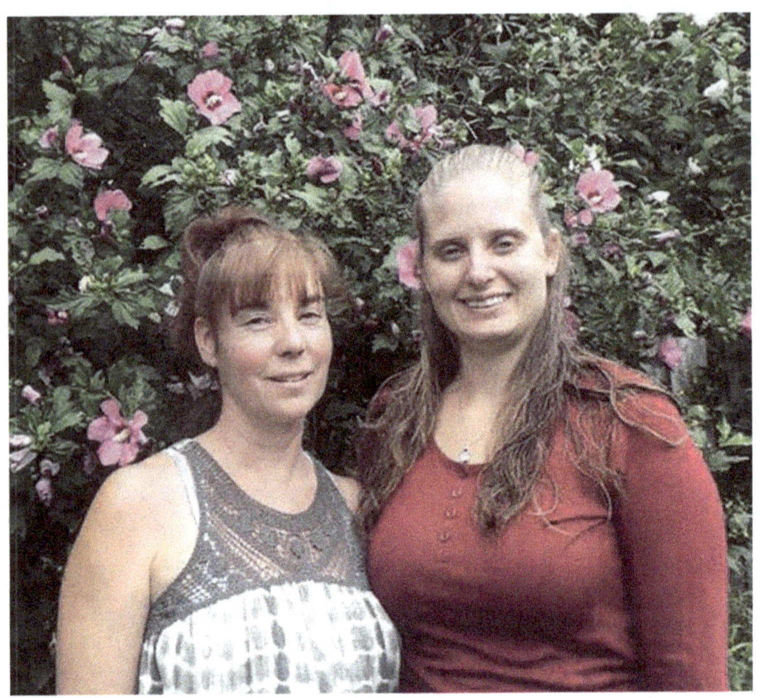

Ashli Couch (Right)

Owner of Bubbles 'n Stitches, her own little crafting business where she makes and sells all natural soaps and lotions along with all her woven and knitted items.

Ashli is self-taught in hand knitting (2011), machine knitting (2018) all natural soaps (2014), lotions (2015), yarn dying (2017), and felting (2017). She learned spinning (2012), frame loom weaving (2012), and peg loom weaving (2017) from Theresa.

Most days you can find Ashli loading up on tea, knitting, weaving, making soap, appeasing her kitties, and working hard on the next weaving book with Theresa.

Theresa Jewell (Left)

Co-Owner of Stone Mountain Looms and Stoney Meadows Alpacas Farm with her husband Chuck Jewell. All the patterns found in this book are of Theresa's design, Ashli just helped her get them on paper.

Theresa is a self-taught yarn artist and has continued to learn and inspire others. Her knowledge of yarn crafts includes: spinning (2002), yarn dying (2002), frame loom weaving (2003), peg loom weaving (2009), tapestry loom weaving (2017), crochet, and felting.

Most days you can find Theresa at her farm taking care of her 'yarn babies' aka her alpaca and sheep or playing with yarn and coming up with more patterns to share in the next book. She also keeps her husband Chuck on his toes by requesting new shaped looms to add to their ever growing collection.

Meet the Maker
(Well, our LOOM maker)

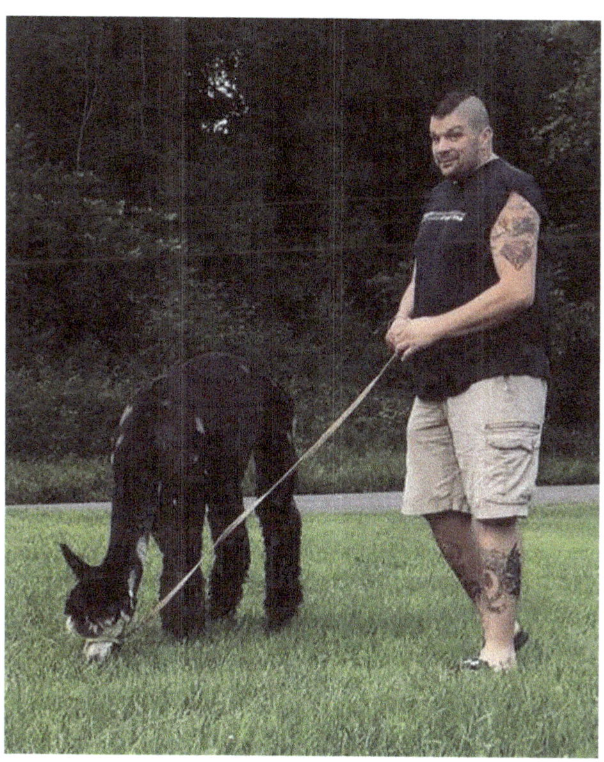

Chuck Jewell

Co-Owner of Stone Mountain Looms and Stoney Meadows Alpacas Farm with his wife Theresa Jewell. Chuck built all the looms showcased in this book.

Chuck was a professional kick boxer when he met Theresa and became involved with the farm. With no woodworking experience, he and Theresa purchased Stone Mountain Looms, received a crash course in making looms, and the rest is history. Since 2017, Chuck continues to improve his woodworking skills by creating new shaped looms for Theresa and occasionally Ashli.